SEINFELD AND ECONOMICS

As the most successful sitcom of all time, the television series *Seinfeld* provides a rich environment for learning basic economic principles. Chronicling the lives of four close friends—Jerry, George, Elaine, and Kramer—the show highlights human behavior at its best and its worst.

The major characters paint themselves as some of the most self-interested individuals in all of popular culture, and are faced with dilemmas that force them to make decisions. Those decisions are at the heart of economics. Each chapter in this book explores one or more key economic concepts and relates them to key scenes from the show. These principles are then applied to other real-world situations, arming readers with the tools needed to make better economic decisions.

Written in a light-hearted and conversational style, this book is a must-read for fans of *Seinfeld* and anyone who wants to learn something from "the show about nothing." It is an ideal supplement for all economics classes.

Linda S. Ghent is Professor of Economics at Eastern Illinois University, U.S.A.

Alan P. Grant is Professor of Economics at Baker University, U.S.A.

ROUTLEDGE ECONOMICS AND POPULAR CULTURE

Series Editor: J. Brian O'Roark, *Robert Morris University, USA*

Broadway and Economics
Economic Lessons from Show Tunes
Matthew C. Rousu

Dystopia and Economics
A Guide to Surviving Everything from the Apocalypse to Zombies
Edited by Charity-Joy Revere Acchiardo and Michelle Albert Vachris

Contemporary Film and Economics
Lights! Camera! Econ!
Samuel R. Staley

Superheroes and Economics
The Shadowy World of Capes, Masks and Invisible Hands
Edited by J. Brian O'Roark and Rob Salkowitz

The Beatles and Economics
Entrepreneurship, Innovation, and the Making of a Cultural Revolution
Samuel R. Staley

War Movies and Economics
Lessons from Hollywood's Adaptations of Military Conflict
Edited by Laura J. Ahlstrom and Franklin G. Mixon, Jr.

Seinfeld **and Economics**
Lessons on Everything from the Show about Nothing
Linda S. Ghent and Alan P. Grant

For more information about this series, please visit www.routledge.com/Routledge-Economics-and-Popular-Culture-Series/book-series/REPC

SEINFELD AND ECONOMICS

Lessons on Everything from the Show about Nothing

Linda S. Ghent and Alan P. Grant

LONDON AND NEW YORK

First published 2021
by Routledge
2 Park Square, Milton Park, Abingdon, Oxon OX14 4RN

and by Routledge
52 Vanderbilt Avenue, New York, NY 10017

Routledge is an imprint of the Taylor & Francis Group, an informa business

© 2021 Linda S. Ghent and Alan P. Grant

The right of Linda S. Ghent and Alan P. Grant to be identified as authors of this work has been asserted by them in accordance with sections 77 and 78 of the Copyright, Designs and Patents Act 1988.

All rights reserved. No part of this book may be reprinted or reproduced or utilized in any form or by any electronic, mechanical, or other means, now known or hereafter invented, including photocopying and recording, or in any information storage or retrieval system, without permission in writing from the publishers.

Trademark notice: Product or corporate names may be trademarks or registered trademarks, and are used only for identification and explanation without intent to infringe.

British Library Cataloguing-in-Publication Data
A catalogue record for this book is available from the British Library

Library of Congress Cataloging-in-Publication Data
A catalog record has been requested for this book

ISBN: 978-0-367-22292-5 (hbk)
ISBN: 978-0-367-22293-2 (pbk)
ISBN: 978-0-429-27430-5 (ebk)

Typeset in Bembo
by Taylor & Francis Books

CONTENTS

1 I cannot spare a square: Scarcity, trade-offs, and opportunity cost   1

2 Mastering your domain: Cost–benefit analysis and incentives   8

3 Ending world hunger: The gains from exchange   16

4 No soup for you: How market structure alters your choices   23

5 Low flow? I don't like the sound of that: Interference in the market   30

6 My rods and cones are all screwed up! Living with externalities   37

7 I am gonna beat the hell out of this car: Markets with asymmetric information   49

8 A man without hand is not a man: Strategic behavior   56

9 $182 is nothing to sneeze at: Are people always rational and is rationality the best thing?   68

Epilogue: You've read the book and yada…yada…yada…, you're now an economist!   75

Index   76

1

I CANNOT SPARE A SQUARE

Scarcity, trade-offs, and opportunity cost

> *Scene: A public restroom. Elaine, having used the facilities, finds that her stall has no toilet paper. Distressed, she calls to a neighboring stall asking for help. But the occupant, Jane, refuses: She can't spare even a single square. Things are getting dire in Elaine's stall. She begs Jane to peel off just a single ply. But her desperate plea is met with anger—Jane can't spare a square and she won't peel a ply.*

As economists, we often are asked by new acquaintances questions like, "You must know a lot about money, huh?" and "What's the stock market going to do?" So you might be wondering what value a book that opens with a dispute over toilet paper could possibly have in answering those questions. It's true, there are many economists who study money and follow financial markets closely. But the vast majority of the economists we know are far more interested in studying things like the health-care system, crime, the craft beer explosion, and, yes, even the market for toilet paper.

If you haven't ever studied economics before, you might be wondering what economics actually *is*. As 19th century economist Alfred Marshall suggests, economics is "a study of mankind in the ordinary business of life." At its heart, economics is about people—their decisions, their behavior, and their foibles. Most economists are interested in why people do the things they do, and what (if anything) we can learn from them to better understand their behavior. Studying economics also teaches individuals the principles of good decision-making; with a little bit of economic know-how, a person can improve his lot in life.

The television series *Seinfeld* is a rich environment for learning basic economic principles. The show, a chronicle of the lives of four close friends, highlights human behavior at its best and at its worst. In episode after episode, the four major characters—Jerry, George, Elaine, and Kramer—are faced with dilemmas that force them to make decisions. And decision-making, remember, is at the heart of economic science. Further, one of the key tenets of economics is that individuals are self-interested. And in all of popular culture, it would be hard to find four people more interested in themselves than Jerry, George, Elaine, and Kramer. For these reasons, *Seinfeld* provides a natural setting for discussions of economic theory.

In this book's opening scene, Elaine's predicament illustrates the two interrelated principles that form the foundation for all of economics. The first of those principles is scarcity. As humans, we have virtually unlimited wants. But because of scarcity—scarcity of time, of money, of talent, of will—we are forced to try to satisfy those unlimited wants with limited means. Elaine wants more toilet paper, but Jane has none to spare—they cannot share the same square of toilet paper. Because of scarcity, only Jane's needs are met; Elaine is left without.

What things are scarce? The easiest way to determine if something is scarce is to ask the following question: If it was free, would there be any left? If the answer is "no," then the item is scarce. So that means that, for something to be non-scarce, it has to be abundant enough that we can't even give it away.

As we see in "The Stall," even though toilet paper may be plentiful in many places, it can become scarce. In times when toilet paper is scarce, people may search for an alternative. During a 2008 economic crisis in Zimbabwe, the government was printing so much money to pay its bills that the country's paper currency became virtually worthless. People started using money *as* toilet paper instead of using it to *buy* toilet paper. The Zimbabwean dollar actually became less scarce than toilet paper!

As you can imagine, there aren't many things in our world that aren't scarce. And, as our discussion above implies, scarcity depends on two things: How much of an item is available, and how badly people want it. Things that are both rare and highly desired are the scarcest of all. And, generally speaking, the more scarce something is, the more valuable it is. This is why diamonds, which are pure carbon, cost a great deal more than charcoal (also pure carbon). This also explains a paradox that has puzzled economics students for generations: Why is water (something we actually need to survive) so much cheaper than diamonds (something pretty, but hardly necessary)? The answer is scarcity: Water is so abundant, and diamonds are so rare! The table below provides some additional examples of things, sorted by their desirability and availability. Those in the upper left are the most scarce, while those in the bottom right are likely not to be scarce at all.

	Highly desired	*Not so desired*
Rare	Diamonds Tom Brady's skill under pressure True love Good boss	Anthrax spores Hailstones Fugu Jalapeno wine Mean dogs
Widely available	Clean water (in the developed world) Hamburger flippers Potato chips Chocolate	Spam email Common cold virus Fruitcake Ticks Psy's "Gangnam Style"

And that brings us to the crux of what economics is really about—not which direction the stock market is headed, or whether the Federal Reserve will increase interest rates, but how we humans can stretch our scarce resources to best satisfy our unlimited wants. Individuals, of course, have to do this all the time—even your authors, who are trained professionals, often find themselves with too much month left at the end of their money or too much to do at the end of their day. And what's true for individuals and households is also true for businesses and governments, who perpetually struggle with the tension of doing more with less.

Without scarcity, there would be no need to economize; economics as we know it would not exist. But scarcity is the rule rather than the exception, and this means that individuals, households, businesses, and governments have to make choices between alternatives—they face trade-offs. To get one thing you like, you often have to give up something else you'd also like. Economists say this means that *"there ain't no such thing as a free lunch."* (Strangely enough, economists have actually created an acronym for this, TANSTAAFL. Say that out loud three times really fast; it's a mouthful!) Sure, your best friend can offer to buy you lunch, but that still doesn't make the lunch "free." After all, you have to take the time to go—that's a cost. No doubt there are other uses for your time. You could be working, shopping, or even taking a nap. You might have other lunch offers to choose from; going to lunch with your friend means you cannot go to lunch with your partner at the same time. You might not particularly enjoy the company of the person buying you lunch—that's a cost, too! Or perhaps your friend is a scorekeeper: "I bought your lunch this time; next time it's your turn to pay." That implies some future cost for you. Those future costs might also crop up in unexpected ways: After stuffing yourself at the all-you-can-eat buffet, you might feel obliged to run off some of your bloat on the treadmill later in the day.

But even if the restaurant is giving away lunches and you had nothing but boredom planned for the lunch hour, it is still the case that costly resources will be used to produce that lunch, such as the ingredients that go into it and the labor used to produce it. Thus, that "free" lunch is, in fact, not free at all. There's a difference, after all, between "free" and "free for you."

> *Scene: Jerry's fellow comedian Kenny Bania has been working out, and his Armani suit doesn't fit anymore. He offers it to Jerry, and the lure of free is too good to pass up. But Bania recognizes the opportunity for a quid pro quo: He suggests Jerry buy him a meal, pointing out that a dinner for a suit is still a great deal. Backed into a corner, Jerry accepts.*

Jerry learns a hard lesson in this scene from "The Soup." He doesn't like Bania, not one bit. After Bania leaves, Jerry wastes no time telling Kramer exactly how he feels: He doesn't want to go to dinner with Bania, not for any reason. In fact, Jerry so dislikes Bania that he tells Kramer he'd rather make his *own* suit. Ironically, Jerry learns the law of no free lunches via the lesson of no free suits.

Economists have a way of measuring these trade-offs called opportunity cost. The opportunity cost of something is what you give up when you choose to do something; it's the value of your next best alternative. That lunch with your friend? Your opportunity cost is what you would be doing if you hadn't actually gone. Any time you make a choice, you incur an opportunity cost.

It should be no surprise that opportunity costs are often measurable in dollars. When you spend $50 on a Swedish massage, you lose the chance to spend that $50 on anything else—the opportunity cost of the massage is what you might have purchased instead.

But, keep in mind that there are many costs out there, and that not all costs are or can be measured in dollars. One big opportunity cost is time. Lunch with a friend—even with a friend who pays—costs you time that you could have spent watching *Seinfeld* reruns. Jerry learns this lesson firsthand in "The Chinese Restaurant:"

> *Scene: Plan 9 from Outer Space is playing at a nearby theater. It's a cult classic, and it's showing for one night only. Jerry doesn't want to miss it! But Jerry's Uncle Leo has asked him to dinner. Torn between dinner with an overbearing uncle and seeing what might possibly be the worst movie ever made, he comes to the only reasonable decision: He feigns illness to escape the dinner invitation and heads for the theater.*

Opportunity costs are also prevalent in relationships. While most people don't think of economists as particularly schmoopy people, they have a lot of good advice to offer others where love and dating are concerned. When Elaine and Jerry try to rekindle their romance in "The Deal," they know that a romantic relationship might well ruin their friendship. To avoid that, they craft a set of carefully constructed rules that they believe will allow them to be both friends and lovers. But George understands opportunity cost and the law of no free lunches. Incredulous, he asks Jerry what alternative universe he thinks he's living in. For all of recorded history, he tells Jerry, man has been trying to come up with a workable friends-with-benefits arrangement, and not once has it been successful. After browbeating Jerry for thinking *he* is the one who's going to unlock the mystery, George issues his final verdict: It can't be done. And George is right, it can't: The deal falls apart.

Romantic relationships almost always require hard choices. Committing to one special person means forgoing the chance to find another special someone who might be even better. Jerry faces this situation in "The Switch."

> *Scene: Jerry's girlfriend doesn't find his humor funny. But his girlfriend's roommate laughs at everything he says. And the roommate also possesses other ... attributes ... that appeal to Jerry's more superficial instincts. Drawn to her, Jerry shares his woes with George, and asks for advice on how to make the switch from dating one roommate to dating the other. Aghast, George tells him to forget the idea and never mention it again: The roommate switch can't be done, has never been done. It's such a heinous act that men have been imprisoned for merely suggesting it.*

Once again, George is trying to be the voice of reason. He tries to tell Jerry that going after the roommate will leave Jerry with neither woman. The opportunity cost of following his heart may be quite large.

The lessons we learn about opportunity cost from *Seinfeld* can help us make better sense of the real world. In 2013, New York City's Metropolitan Transportation Authority suspended subway service on the B and Q lines for almost two hours while workers labored to rescue a pair of stray kittens that had been spotted on the tracks. Eventually, the search was called off and service was resumed. (The kittens were found safe and sound several hours later.)

Those were two very expensive kittens! Don't get us wrong, we have nothing against cuddly kittens. (Nothing, that is, except that they're not puppies.) And it's not like they spent a lot of *money* trying to rescue the fuzzy bundles of love. But remember that costs don't have to be measured in dollars. Here, the real cost was borne by thousands of commuters who found themselves stranded for hours and who lost opportunities as a result. They lost time at work, they missed job interviews, and they missed time with their families. Suppose Jasmine, a print shop owner, was on the train to go and open her store for the day. The delay potentially costs her business; customers stop by and they find her store closed, so they simply go to her competitor's shop instead. But the costs don't stop there. Makayla and Malcolm, two advertising executives, are gearing up for a presentation to their clients, and have stopped by Jasmine's shop to pick up the posters and brochures they developed. But, Jasmine is stuck at the train station, so Makayla and Malcolm are unable to get their materials. They, too, are forced to bear the costs of the shutdown. There are likely countless stories just like these. The decision to stop the trains, even for only two hours, can have far-reaching impacts and impose costs on individuals who were nowhere near the trains that morning.

Here's the irony: While thousands of commuters waited as workers searched for two stray felines in the subway, in the very same city (and in many other cities across the country), workers at animal shelters were euthanizing stray kittens! If society is really interested in having two more kittens, the economist's solution would be to keep the trains running and euthanize two fewer kittens at the animal shelter. (The fact that economists point this out is one reason why economists are seldom invited to dinner parties.)

Nobody gets to violate the law of no free lunches. Everyone—people, businesses, governments—all operate under conditions of scarcity. Even the United States government, with a federal budget of over $4 trillion, can't do everything it wants—it must make choices. This is why Republicans and Democrats in Washington, D.C. are always arguing about how costly government programs are, or how big the next tax cut will be. They want to provide everything that makes their voters happy. But, there simply aren't enough financial resources to do that— this is why our government often has to borrow money to pay its bills.

And because our government can't have it all, it needs to carefully evaluate its choices. Building a $20 billion border wall to keep out immigrants has a very real opportunity cost—for the same money, we could build not one, but almost TWO new aircraft carriers. Which of these choices would do the most to keep America secure? That is the question our leaders need to ask (and we will address how they could answer that question in Chapter 2).

What about building a space force? In 2018, President Trump suggested that we need an additional armed force, on equivalent footing with the army, navy, air force, marines, and coast guard. The estimated cost? "Only" $13 billion for the first five years! What else could the U.S. government use this money for? Think about the programs typically decried as underfunded: Education; veterans' medical care; new roads and highways (or fixing the ones already in existence!); national parks; scientific research; the arts. Or, perhaps the government will have to choose between the border wall and the space force.

We see the importance of opportunity cost when we look at the costs of a college education. Generally speaking, the costs are of two types: Explicit and implicit costs. Explicit costs are costs that we actually see; we can examine the individual's checking account or credit card statements and watch these costs accrue.

Here's a sample accounting of the explicit costs of a college education:[1]

Tuition:	$12,000
Books:	$1,000
Lab equipment:	$600
Beer pong supplies:	$850
Annual total	**$14,450**
x6 years	**$86,700**

So, a college education looks pretty pricey. But, we haven't even talked about the implicit costs of college. Implicit costs are basically opportunity costs; we don't pay for them outright, but they affect us nonetheless. The most important opportunity cost of attending college is the value of the student's *time* while he is in school. What else could he be doing rather than going to school? Our guess is that he would be working full time! In some states he could earn as much as $15 per hour flipping burgers! That's at least $30,000 per year, or $180,000 in the six years it might take him to earn his degree.

As we just saw, the implicit costs of college far outweigh the explicit costs. And, the greater your potential earnings without a degree, the more expensive college becomes. There is a good reason why talented athletes decide to leave college before completing their degree to become professionals. For example, in the 2018 NBA draft, many of the top first-round picks were college freshmen who opted to go pro after completing only one year of college. Why would they choose to do this? For these athletes, the opportunity cost of going to college is very, very high. Their most valuable resources, their time and their talents, were not being valued in college as highly as they would be in the NBA. Going to college might be pricey for all of us, but for these young men, it can cost millions of dollars. Staying in college would require them to forgo huge salaries and run the risk of getting injured, lowering their future value to the league. Of course, choosing the NBA implies an opportunity cost as well—the player must forgo finishing his degree for the time being. Many players do eventually finish their schooling but must do so in the off-season or after they retire. Michael Jordan, Shaquille O'Neal, and Antawn Jamison are great examples of players who left college early to enter the NBA, only to return to college later to fulfill their degree requirements. But they couldn't simultaneously attend school and play in the NBA. Scarcity means we can't have it all.

It seems that Jerry, George, and Elaine can teach us two very important lessons: First, because of scarcity, we must choose among competing opportunities. And second, every opportunity we choose implies an alternative opportunity foregone. Evaluating those trade-offs is the essence of economics. So, the next time a political candidate tells you that you can have it all, remember TANSTAAFL! Or (because remembering that mouthful may just impose too large a cost on you) just mutter to yourself, "…no free lunch, no free lunch, no free lunch…"

Note

1 Some might include room and board (but economists might argue that the individual needs a roof and food even if he doesn't attend college).

2

MASTERING YOUR DOMAIN

Cost–benefit analysis and incentives

*Scene: George's mother has caught him in a compromising situation in the bathroom, with a copy of her Glamour magazine and too much time on his hands. Later, describing his woes to his friends over coffee, George vows that he will never do **that** again. Jerry doesn't think George has the kind of restraint it takes to stop. George doesn't believe that Jerry could refrain from ... that ... either and suggests a bet. Within minutes, a contest is underway. Kramer wants in, too. By the time they leave the diner, all four friends have contributed $100 to a winner-take-all pot to see who can hold out the longest.*

People do some strange things. Rarely a day goes by when we don't see someone doing something that makes us go, "What on Earth?!" And yet, the things people choose to do may, and probably do, make perfect sense to them. Why do they choose these things? Economists believe that individuals make decisions by comparing the costs and benefits of any particular action: Simply, individuals choose to undertake activities for which the benefits are at least as large as the costs. Jerry, George, Elaine, and Kramer rarely deny themselves anything. But in this chapter's opening scene from "The Contest," they uncharacteristically deny themselves something they find particularly pleasurable. Why? Because the chance of winning a $400 bet is worth more to them than the pleasure they are forgoing. Of course, they also likely to be able to brag.

It is the bet that drives them to deny themselves ... except that some end up caring less about the $400 than the alternative. As "The Contest" unfolds, the four friends fall like dominoes. Kramer has the least self-control, and is the first one out. George quickly follows. With only himself and Elaine remaining, Jerry is poised for victory. But when a beautiful woman in the apartment across the street begins undressing in front of her window, Jerry's cost–benefit calculations change.

Kramer, who is already out of the contest, can't wait to watch; Jerry does everything he can to *avoid* watching. For Kramer, the benefits of seeing the naked woman far outweigh the costs. But Jerry would rather win the bet than yield to the temptation the woman poses. Both Kramer and Jerry are selecting the option for which the benefits outweigh the costs—from an economist's standpoint, they are both correct. Good decision-makers never purposefully make themselves worse off. Of course, sometimes the costs and benefits of a decision are uncertain, so not all decisions turn out to be good ones—just ask anyone who invested in Enron.

As we discovered in Chapter 1, costs aren't just monetary in nature. Neither are benefits. The fact is that decision-makers must often compare costs and benefits that are quite subjective and implicit in nature. But we do it all of the time. The alarm goes off in the morning. Do you hit the snooze button? Sure, an extra nine minutes of sleep is amazing, but that comes at a cost. You may be late to work, or rush out of the house with mismatched shoes. Only you can decide if the benefits of those extra nine minutes of shuteye are worth the costs. If you hit that snooze button, we'll assume that you believe they are.

One key rule is to ignore costs that have already been incurred and are not recoverable. Economists call these "sunk costs." It's important to recognize that you'll never be able to recoup sunk costs no matter how hard you try—in the words of a viral internet meme, "Don't cling to your mistakes just because you spent a long time making them."

Unfortunately, people have a hard time ignoring sunk costs. Farmers harvest their crops even when the value of the crop won't cover the cost of the harvest. "I've planted the crop—it would be foolish not to bring it in." Investors refuse to sell nearly worthless stocks because "I paid $50 per share five years ago." And how many of you know someone who clung to a relationship that was clearly going nowhere because "We've been together for years; we've got so much *history?*" Each of these examples is fraught with bad economic decision-making.

Elaine learns the lesson of sunk costs the hard way in "The Strike:"

> Scene: Elaine has purchased 23 mediocre sandwiches at Atomic Subs, and with each bad sandwich has gotten a stamp on a special card. She's anxious to get her 24th stamp, which will earn her the title of "Submarine Captain" and reward her with a free sub. Unfortunately, she loses her card. This sends her into a tailspin—she wants that free sandwich that she "earned." Jerry tells her not to worry about it, after all, she'd walk out of a bad movie, wouldn't she?

Elaine knows that the subs are bad, but she still insists on going to get her "free" sub. (You already know THAT doesn't exist!) She is considering the cost she has already borne (the 23 bad subs) in making her decision to go and get another. But, those subs are already eaten; she can't go back and change the decisions she made to suffer through them. She can, however, save herself from eating another. She should ask herself, "Is it worth eating another even if I don't have to pay for it?" rather than telling herself, "I've invested by buying 23 bad subs—I must eat another to make those 23 subs worth it!" Those 23 subs are a sunk cost. Elaine should just follow Jerry's advice and stop worrying about the sandwich.

Jerry, who has shown his economic mojo in advising Elaine to ignore sunk costs, must also consider costs and benefits in "The Baby Shower:"

> Scene: The cable companies are in a legal dispute, and Jerry has had to resort to using a TV antenna to watch his favorite shows. Kramer tries to convince him to install illegal cable. But Jerry is worried about getting caught and is fearful that sirens and bells will sound when he turns his television on. Kramer then informs Jerry that the New York Mets will have 75 games on cable that year. That information seals the deal.

Jerry's hesitation to install illegal cable results from a cost–benefit decision: Is the benefit of being able to watch my favorite shows worth the risk of getting caught? Apparently, the answer is no. Jerry's vision of the cops breaking down his door to arrest him imposes too high a cost for him to agree to the illegal hookup. Once Kramer tells him about the Mets, however, the benefits of installing illegal cable rise, pushing them higher than the costs. That swings Jerry's decision and the cable is installed.

While individuals might be less likely to install illegal cable these days, we do see another version of cable pirating occurring, the sharing of streaming service accounts (like Netflix, HULU and HBOGO) across individuals in different households. In fact, a 2017 Reuters poll revealed that 12 percent of adults surveyed admitted that they had accessed a streaming service using login credentials that belonged to people outside their household. That number rises to 21 percent for those aged 18 to 24. This clearly violates the user agreements of these services. So, why is it so pervasive? Remember that people take actions when the benefits of those actions are at least as large as the costs. In this case, the benefits of sharing (more variety, access to popular shows) far outweigh the costs of getting caught. This is especially true because it is apparent to all that these streaming services are not actively pursuing violators.

Another way to think about this issue is to consider the incentives involved. We like to think that we have free will, that we are making our own (sometimes ridiculous-seeming) choices. But the truth is, there are puppet masters everywhere shaping our decisions, nudging us to make choices that we otherwise might not.

They do this by shaping our incentives. Incentives are things that move us to behave in a particular way. Incentives work by altering individuals' cost–benefit calculations so that they behave in ways they might otherwise not. Understanding what someone's motivations are and what incentives he faces can be a valuable tool in predicting … and altering … that person's choices. And because economics is all about how people make choices under conditions of scarcity (if you don't remember that, you'd better go back and read Chapter 1 again!), incentives are super-important. This is why economist Steven Landsburg asserts, "Most of economics can be summarized in four words: 'People respond to incentives.' The rest is commentary."

One way incentives can change behavior is by increasing the benefits of engaging in activities we otherwise wouldn't. In "The Contest," George, Jerry, Kramer, and Elaine would be unlikely to exercise such personal restraint in the absence of any benefit. In this case, the chance of winning a $400 bet serves as a "carrot" (or positive incentive) to behave in a less ... self-interested ... fashion.

Similar carrots pop up every day to encourage us to engage in activities we'd rather not. One of the biggest and most pervasive incentives we face is in prices. When Kohl's wants to clear its Christmas and winter items for swimsuits and short-sleeved shirts, it doesn't offer its customers cookies and milk; it simply discounts the price of its winter line until the racks clear.

Employers use incentives when they give bonuses to particularly productive employees, or compensate those employees on a commission basis: The more you sell, the more you make! These compensation schemes get employees to work harder than they otherwise might. (Have you ever wondered why your employer wants you to own some of the firm's stock, and may even help you buy it?)

Sometimes the government encourages people to behave in particular ways by paying them—or by giving them a tax credit—to engage in particular activities. Buy a hybrid automobile or install solar panels in your home, and the government might give you a tax credit. In fact, some governments even give parents a tax credit for having children! And because (in the U.S.) you get an entire year's worth of tax credit even if your child is born on the last day of the year, there are a lot of extra births in the week before January 1, and a disproportionately small number in the week after. (Whether this is because parents choose to induce labor earlier rather than later or whether they are paying doctors to falsify birth certificates is a matter of pure speculation!)

Insurance companies often craft incentives to convince people to behave in desirable ways. Life and health insurers offer discounts to non-smokers. In a similar fashion, auto insurers offer safe-driver discounts to those who haven't gotten a ticket or had an accident in the past several years. Auto and home insurers will also offer you a discount if you sign up for multiple policies from the same insurer.

One big truth is that whatever can be accomplished with a carrot can also be accomplished with a stick. In other words, you can *discourage* undesirable behaviors by increasing the cost of those behaviors. Consider auto safety: While you can get drivers to be more careful by offering discounts to safe drivers, you can accomplish the same thing by increasing the cost of driving recklessly. Economist Gordon Tullock once suggested that we could reduce auto deaths to almost zero by removing seatbelts and airbags and replacing them with a spike mounted in the center of the steering column. (Have we mentioned that economists make spectacular dinner party guests?)

Of course, not all "sticks" come in the form of spikes. One big, blunt stick comes in the form of taxes. Governments use tax policy to discourage all kinds of behaviors that society (or legislators) believe are undesirable. The U.S. government heavily taxes "undesirable" activities like smoking—in Chicago, Illinois, the combined tax on a pack of cigarettes (at the federal, state, and local levels) is $7.42. The government can increase prices in other ways, too. For example, in Scotland, the leading cause of illness and early death is alcohol. To discourage heavy drinking, the Scottish local government recently mandated above-market minimum prices for distilled spirits—the higher the alcohol content, the greater the price increase. Those price controls raised the price of booze by up to 90 percent in some cases!

Whether they appear in the form of carrots or sticks, incentives can be found in households too. Parents give their children financial rewards or sugary treats when they study hard and get good grades. A teenager who cleans his room may get the internet password for the day or be allowed additional screen time. These are rewards to incentivize desirable behavior. On the other hand, misbehaving may lead to punishments, such as being grounded or having a favorite toy taken away.

Individuals may also use incentives to enhance their love lives. A new website, WhatsYourPrice.com, offers financial incentives to go on first dates. Individuals list the amount they believe their time is worth, and others can bid for a date. The average price, according to the website, is $125.

Of course, the romantic incentive with the most tradition surrounding it is the diamond engagement ring. Since the early 1900s, men have been offering women diamonds in exchange for a promise to marry. Economist Margaret Brinig, though, argues that men's motives were more underhanded. She claims (and backs that claim with statistics) that prior to the sexual revolution of the 1960s, men offered women of virtue diamond engagement rings to motivate their participation in decidedly *unvirtuous* premarital behaviors. The lesson on incentives still applies.

Elaine experiences just such a situation in "The Wig Master:"

> *Scene: While shopping with Jerry in an expensive clothing store, Elaine meets Craig, a sales clerk. Craig tells Elaine that he can get her a discount on the black, sleeveless Nicole Miller dress she is coveting. Elaine asks why he's willing to help her, pointing out that she barely knows him. He replies that they should get to know each other better, then. When she tells Jerry about the exchange, he sees right through Craig's generous offer, pointing out that Craig is going to dangle the discount in front of Elaine as an incentive for her to date him. On the other hand, Kramer sees the incentive working the opposite direction; Elaine is only interested in being nice to Craig so she can receive the Nicole Miller dress at a steep discount.*

Elaine and Craig each want something from the other. Craig obviously doesn't give a discount to just anyone, so Elaine uses her feminine wiles to entice him to offer one to her. Elaine normally wouldn't be interested in dating a man like Craig, but the opportunity to get a discount on a dress by her favorite designer is enough to make her feign interest. They each use an incentive to persuade the other to give them what they want. And, by changing the costs or benefits in some way, they can alter each other's decisions to achieve what they want.

We might even provide incentives to ourselves to nudge our own behavior. Have you ever wanted to get rid of a bad habit or start a new healthy one? For example, you may promise yourself a reward if you finish that next 30 minutes of exercise, or if you can lose 10 pounds. And, if you stay true to yourself, you will only allow yourself the reward once you've met your goal. Of course, it's easy to cheat; after all, you meant well when setting the goal, so it's okay if you miss it but get *close*.

To keep this from happening, you can turn to stickk.com, a website developed by two economists who understand that people respond to incentives. On this site, you enter into a "commitment contract," where you will pay money to someone (or some organization) if you do not complete your goal. You also assign someone to monitor your progress. This is a way to incentivize you (using a stick) if you do not complete your goal. Of course, the result depends on how you set up the contract. If you agree to pay the Humane Society $100 if you don't meet your goal, and you love animals, the incentive effects of the contract will not be as strong as it would if you had agreed to send the same $100 to an organization you hate. Stickk.com has created hundreds of thousands of contracts with millions of dollars on the line. People are willingly putting their money at risk to help themselves achieve their goals!

Another website devoted to helping individuals lose weight and exercise more is healthywage.com. On this site, individuals make a personal weight loss bet or enter into exercise challenges for money. The weight loss bet spans a six-month period, and the cash prize is determined both by how much weight the individuals are betting to lose and how much money they are willing to wager. The healthywage website is full of success stories—people who claim that it was the financial incentive that got them to (finally!) lose the weight. Apparently the distant threat of future health issues like heart disease isn't enough of an incentive—but the immediate threat of losing money is!

Okay, sure—ordinary people respond to incentives. But what about criminals? We already discussed the installation of illegal cable and the sharing of streaming service passwords above. But what about serious crimes? Don't you have to be an irrational, crazy person to commit a murder? Surely irrational, crazy people don't respond to incentives in the same way ordinary people do, right?

Let's suppose a potential criminal spies an iPhone Z in the back seat of a parked car. Two factors a rational criminal might include in a cost–benefit analysis of whether it's worth breaking into the car to steal the iPhone are the likelihood of getting caught and the severity of the punishment if he does get caught. The greater the likelihood of getting caught, or the more severe the punishment, the less crime we should see, *provided that criminals are rational!* If, on the other hand, criminals are acting on impulse or are simply dedicated to sowing chaos and doing evil, then they won't undertake a rational cost–benefit analysis; the certainty and severity of punishment won't affect their behavior at all.

So, do criminals respond to incentives? A bunch of economists have shown that, in fact, they do. Thomas Marvell and Carlisle Moody gathered 20 years of data from a number of cities and determined that increasing the number of police in a city (and therefore increasing the likelihood of getting caught should you commit a crime) by ten percent causes the overall crime rate to fall by three percent. In other words, people are more likely to commit crimes when the chance of getting caught is lower. And how about the severity of punishment? Economist Steven Levitt showed that criminals respond predictably to the severity of punishment by comparing crime rates for juveniles near age 18 (for whom punishments are generally limited) and adults just over age 18 (for whom criminal behavior can be punished more severely). Not surprisingly, criminal activity falls once a person hits age 18, and it falls the most in states where the difference in punishment between juveniles and adults is the largest. In other words, society isn't simply powerless to protect itself from a collection of crazed supercriminals; even criminals respond rationally to the swift and certain application of "the stick."

Sometimes, incentives align nicely with goals that society generally finds desirable. For example, lots of people want the economy to create lots of wealth. At the same time, those same people want businesses to deliver that wealth to consumers in the form of high-quality, low-cost products. As it turns out, the capitalist, market-based system that the United States has chosen encourages the greatest possible production to be delivered to consumers at the lowest possible cost. The profit motive inherent in capitalism actually encourages businesses to serve their customers instead of screwing them; in the process, the economic pie increases.

Consider this opening monologue from "The Mango:"

> *Scene: Jerry is doing a stand-up comedy routine at a club, and he's fixated on the seedless watermelon. He points out that some scientists spend their careers fighting diseases such as cancer or AIDS. But others are devoting their careers to producing watermelon without seeds. Jerry seems confused about the value of this work.*

In a way, Jerry is right. Do we really *need* seedless watermelons? Maybe not. But, we *want* them. And we want them enough to pay extra money for them. It is that willingness to pay that offers an incentive to scientists to create those seedless watermelons for us. You see, consumers are sovereign in a market economy. They are the ones who truly determine what gets produced. Why don't we see restaurants serving cockroach sandwiches? Because people won't pay for them. And, if you can't sell something, you aren't going to waste resources producing it.

If you don't provide a product that consumers want, you won't last long in business. Consider this scene from "The Café:"

> *Scene: Jerry finds himself providing business advice to Babu, a restaurant owner. Babu has opened a restaurant near Jerry's apartment called Dream Café. Jerry thinks Babu has made a mistake by offering a variety of cuisines like those in other restaurants around him: Chinese, Mexican, and Italian. Once in the restaurant, Jerry advises him to change the cuisine to Pakistani. Babu is concerned about doing this, because there are very few Pakistanis in the neighborhood. Jerry assures him that everything will work out fine because Babu will have the only Pakistani restaurant in the area. Babu follows Jerry's advice. He borrows money, remodels his restaurant, and converts it to Pakistani cuisine. Unfortunately, nobody comes to eat Babu's Pakistani cuisine. When Jerry stops in for a bite, he discovers that Babu is very angry at him for providing him with such bad business advice.*

What went wrong? It turns out that having the only Pakistani restaurant wasn't a great thing, because no one wanted to eat Pakistani food. Producing a product that no one wants to pay for is a sure-fire path to bankruptcy.

In general, consumers' willingness to pay works as an incentive to producers because prices serve as a great signal in our market economy. Suppose that researchers at the Mayo Clinic discover that eating an ear of corn each day is the fountain of youth. What will happen? Consumers will flock to the store to buy as much corn as they can. This will drive the price of corn up. How will farmers respond? They will plant more corn—which is exactly what consumers want! Ta da! It's magic! Note that it doesn't take an act of Congress to get more corn to the marketplace. The consumers' willingness to pay more is what drives the farmers to plant more corn. You see, the consumer is king after all.

Unfortunately, incentives don't always naturally align with social goals. It's much easier to dump your used motor oil in the alley than to take it to a disposal center; it's cheaper to buy a less-efficient water heater than the energy-efficient tankless style. In both cases, individuals may make choices that impose costs on others; the economic pie may shrink rather than grow. So governments often craft policies to help align individual incentives with social goals. They subsidize efficient water heaters and furnaces; they require parents to vaccinate their children; they tax firms who pollute our air and water.

As you might have gleaned from the discussion above, governments are heavily involved in crafting incentives. Sometimes, those incentives work to motivate citizens to behave in the ways intended. However, government policies can also at times create perverse incentives that were never anticipated by policymakers.

For example, the South African government has a program to help poor, unemployed individuals with disabilities, including AIDS. The government began providing disability grants, where the amount of the payment was determined by how sick the individual was. After all, the sicker the individual, the less likely she will be able to work (especially in an economy with an unemployment rate greater than 25 percent). This well-intentioned policy had a perverse incentive; people were incentivized to become sicker! Individuals stopped taking their AIDS medications, and some even tried to become infected with different strains of the virus. Of course, none of this was really a surprise to economists. Incentives can motivate people to do things that they never would have done otherwise.

This chapter highlighted two very important principles of economics. One is the idea of cost–benefit calculation and the role it plays in our daily lives. A rational person will always (at least implicitly) examine the benefits and costs of a particular action and then choose an action only if its costs are not greater than its benefits. The second principle is how incentives, in the form of rewards (higher benefits) or punishments (higher costs), might alter our cost–benefit calculations and convince us to change our behavior. The key to good public policy (or even to motivating your children to do your bidding) is often found in crafting appropriate incentives. Of course, if the incentives you create prove ineffective in getting an important job done, you may be forced to use a larger carrot … or a bigger stick. Good luck!

3

ENDING WORLD HUNGER

The gains from exchange

Scene: Jerry's girlfriend Karen is Miss Rhode Island. She's about to compete in the Miss America contest, and Kramer has been asked to chaperone. At a dinner before the contest, Kramer puts her through a mock interview, asking what she would do as Miss America to make the world a better place. She replies that she'd like to end world hunger. Her plan? Have every person sacrifice one meal a week, freeing up enough food to feed the world's hungry. Jerry, unimpressed, rolls his eyes and tells her that she's got one hell of a plan.

Remember back in the first chapter, when we said that nothing comes without cost? We lied. Jerry's girlfriend, Karen, believes that the only way to make one person better off is to make someone else worse off. But Jerry, with his tongue-in-cheek endorsement of Karen's scheme to end world hunger, recognizes the truth: One person's win doesn't have to be another person's loss. There's one important thing we all do that makes *everybody* a winner. That one thing is the process of trade and exchange.

How can trade make everyone better off? One way is by rearranging goods among people. Ally likes country music; Juliette likes hip-hop. If Ally receives tickets to a hip-hop music festival as a Christmas gift, and Juliette receives tickets to a country music festival, neither is going to be very happy. But if they *swap* those tickets, both will be happy.

Here's the interesting part of Ally's and Juliette's exchange: The trade creates nothing new to bring the world any additional happiness. Instead, the simple process of rearranging the goods among people has allowed the world to extract more happiness from the same stuff! And, after all, that's what economics is: Figuring out how to get the most value out of scarce resources, whether those resources are bulldozers, the 24 hours in a day, the contents of your wallet, or a couple of sets of concert tickets.

Scene: Kramer has received a gift of Cuban cigars, and has been trading them for access to a country club golf course. After he carelessly burns up his supply of cigars (and a cabin as well!), he appears at the Cuban embassy in search of more. He asks the man who greets him to sell him a couple of boxes. The man shows Kramer a cigar, at the same time commenting how Kramer must surely know that Cuban cigars are illegal in the U.S. While Kramer feigns ignorance, the man reaches out, touches Kramer's lapel, and remarks wistfully how much he likes Kramer's jacket.

Kramer wants to buy Cuban cigars. He and a gentleman from the embassy find an agreeable price—Kramer's jacket. Because Kramer values the cigars more than the jacket, and because the gentleman values the jacket more than the cigars, the two easily find a way to enjoy and share in the gains from exchange. There are no losers: Kramer wins, the gentleman wins. And this trade is entirely voluntary. Each is perfectly happy to give up something that they value for something that they value more.

A similar situation occurs in some Orange County, Florida, elementary schools. These schools have developed "sharing tables." After students get their lunch trays, they can visit this table to leave any items they will not eat and pick up extra servings of items they like. This way, less food goes to waste. Little Aiden doesn't like carrots? No problem. He can drop off his carrots at the sharing table and pick up an extra apple left by someone else. Students get a lunch that provides them with more happiness, and it doesn't cost the school system a penny more.

So, trade can make us better off by simply doing a better job matching existing products and services with the people who want them. But the real power of trade lies in its ability to generate more goods and services for everybody to enjoy. The first person to really understand this power was Adam Smith, a Scottish philosopher who is now widely regarded as the father of modern economics. Smith made an observation that seems so obvious to us today, but which wasn't at all clear in 1776, when he wrote his magnum opus, *The Wealth of Nations*. He noted that if Canadians and Guatemalans both enjoy bananas and maple syrup, it makes little sense to try to grow both bananas and maple trees in both places—it takes a lot of extra effort to grow bananas in Canada, and it takes just as much extra effort to grow sugar maples in Guatemala. It makes far more sense to let Guatemalans grow all the bananas and Canadians make the syrup. This allows both to make better use of their land and their labor; the happy result is more bananas and more syrup for everyone to enjoy! And then, after all the growing is done, Canadians and Guatemalans can simply trade bananas for syrup until they're all stuffed to the uvula with Bananas Foster.

Smith's common-sense revelation about specialization being a huge source of the gains from trade still has traction today. But Smith couldn't answer one very important question: Would there be any reason to trade with Guatemala if Canada was better at growing both bananas and maple trees? (There's a rumor that the absent-minded Smith was once so engrossed in solving this puzzle that he walked straight into an open pit!)

It wasn't until a half-century later that another Brit, David Ricardo, came up with the answer. He showed that the source of the gains from trade didn't stem from who could produce things more quickly and efficiently (as Smith thought), but who could produce them at a lower opportunity cost. Here's how Ricardo's theory works. Suppose Bailey and Diego both love smoothies and baguettes:

- Diego is a capable cook, and in three hours he can either make one smoothie or bake one baguette.
- Bailey is even better—she can make a smoothie in an hour or a baguette in two.

Now, let's imagine that they are holed up in a snowstorm, and for the first day they make nothing but smoothies. Bailey makes 24 smoothies; Diego makes eight. Between them, they've got 32 smoothies, but no bread. The next day, they get the munchies, and decide to make just a single baguette.

Who should make it? It's tempting to say that Bailey should—after all, it only takes her two hours, and it would take Diego three. If Bailey did bake the baguette, at the end of the day the happy couple would have 30 smoothies and one baguette.[1] But look at what happens if Diego makes the baguette instead—Bailey makes 24 smoothies, and Diego makes 7 smoothies and a baguette; the couple ends up sharing 31 smoothies and a baguette.[2] That's one more smoothie than they had to share when super-fast Bailey did the baking. In other words, sometimes it's better to let the slow guy do the work!

How is it that the couple is better off with Diego making the baguette? Notice that in the two hours it takes Bailey to bake a single baguette, she could have made two smoothies. So, the couple loses two smoothies when Bailey bakes the bread (that's the notion of opportunity cost we talked about in Chapter 1). But in the three hours it takes Diego to bake a baguette, he could have only made one smoothie. Assigning the slow guy to bake the baguette minimizes the number of smoothies the couple gives up when they decide they want a crusty French loaf. And what's true for a single baguette is true for any number the couple might want—this couple will be best off if Bailey specializes in making smoothies and, if baguettes are desired, Diego is the one to bake them. The couple can then trade with each other to satisfy their appetites.

In other words, Smith was partially right: Whoever is "best" at producing a product should specialize in producing that product. But it was Ricardo who pointed out that the "best" producer isn't necessarily the fastest one, but the one who can produce at the lowest *opportunity cost*.

As difficult as it may be to understand who should produce what, examining relative opportunity costs has a lot of value to ordinary people like you and me:

> *Scene: Jerry's at the comedy club, doing a bit about how uncomfortable he is with having a maid. He feels guilty sitting idly while someone else is working all around him, and he feels like he should apologize for not cleaning up before she arrived. He remarks that he could never be a maid, because he'd feel nothing but disdain for a person who hires someone else to clean up their own filth—a job they could have done themselves.*

Jerry misses an important lesson here: It's not that he's incapable of vacuuming his own carpets; an understanding of relative opportunity costs tells us that he's simply got a better use of his time. Rather than cleaning his own apartment, he should take that time to write more jokes or take another gig. With the extra money he earns, he can more than pay for another week of maid service! This is exactly why J.K. Rowling shouldn't bake her own bread and Warren Buffett shouldn't do his own taxes.

The beauty of trade is that it allows each of us to specialize in something we are able to produce at a low cost and then trade with others doing something different, providing us all with more of everything. From a societal standpoint, trade is not a zero-sum game; it is a win-win situation every time.

While economists love trade, many others in the world often rail against it. Every day we hear stories of people losing jobs to foreign competition. That must mean trade is a bad thing, right?

Imagine the following: Henri P. Reneur is a smart, friendly Midwesterner. One day, he announces that he's developed a new way to make cars from corn. He builds a gigantic building in Seattle, and production begins—every morning truckloads of corn go in the east door; every evening, trainloads of cars go out the west door. Henri then sells those cars for less than any other automaker.

Henri is hailed as a hero, and he's written up in all the usual rags—the *Wall Street Journal*, *Business Week*, the *Financial Times*. People stop him on the street and praise him for his brilliance. And then, one fateful day, the *National Enquirer* publishes photos of his production process: Under cover of darkness each night, Henri loads corn onto a boat bound for Japan, and unloads a bunch of cars. It turns out that he's not making cars out of corn after all—he's trading the corn for cars made elsewhere! Overnight, Henri is recast as America's biggest villain—he hasn't invented a new and better way to produce cars; he's lining his pockets while stealing jobs from American autoworkers!

Of course, Henri really *has* invented a new technology for car production— harnessing the power of specialization. Instead of producing cars *directly*, by welding steel and melting rubber, Henri's technology allows the United States to produce cars *indirectly*, by tilling fields and planting seeds. David Ricardo tells us that this indirect method of car production makes America wealthier on the whole by allowing us to take advantage of our relatively lower opportunity cost—not in automaking, but in growing corn.

This parable, attributable to economist David Friedman, highlights the political tension that international trade and exchange creates. When autoworkers are thrown out of work by a new production technology—say, robotics—we tend to sympathize with their plight but agree that the gains created by the new technology (such as cheaper and better cars) are worth it. But when autoworkers are thrown out of work by Henri's new indirect technology (which is really the same as a new production technology—more cars from fewer resources), we are often tempted to fight to save those autoworkers' jobs.

The uproar that these job losses create often leads government officials to take measures to limit the amount of trade that occurs. One way they can do this is through the use of tariffs, which are taxes on imported products. The idea is simple: Tariffs raise the price of imported goods, inducing consumers to purchase less of them. But, remember our discussion above. Trade is voluntary, so the consumers buying those imported goods actually wanted to purchase those goods; those transactions made them better off. And trade allows specialization because some producers can make these goods at a lower cost, so production occurs more efficiently. What happens when the government places a tariff on the good? Fewer trades take place. Fewer *voluntary* trades take place. This reduces overall consumer well-being and causes us to use more resources to produce the same products.

Two other things occur when tariffs are placed on imported goods. First, countries often retaliate against one another. When the United States imposes tariffs on Chinese goods, China responds with tariffs on U.S., exports. That hurts U.S. producers. Second, because buyers still want the product, and sellers still want to sell the product, they try to find ways around the law. Consider, for example, the "Chicken Tax." In the 1960s, to protect its farmers from foreign competition from the U.S., Europe placed a tariff on imported chickens. The U.S. responded with tariffs of its own on foreign-made trucks and commercial vans. The target of the tariff was Volkswagen, but several decades later Ford Motor Company found itself affected, too.

You see, Ford makes its Transit Connect vans in Spain and then ships them to the U.S. to be sold. Unfortunately, if these are commercial vans, they will be taxed like any other foreign-made commercial van. So, to avoid the tariff, Ford builds the Transit Connect vans in Spain as passenger vans; they have windows down each side and a back row of seats. Then, once the vans reach the U.S., the rear seats and back windows are removed, and the van gets turned back into a commercial van. What happens to the seats and windows? The fabric is shredded, all of the other parts are broken down, and everything goes off to a recycling center. So, Ford takes raw materials and expends resources to build seats no one will ever sit in and windows no one will ever look out of. Then Ford spends more resources tearing out those seats and windows and turning them back into raw materials. Does that sound like an efficient use of our scarce resources to you?

What does Ford gain by doing this? Because the tariff on foreign-produced commercial vans is a whopping 25 percent, while the tariff on passenger vehicles is only 2.5 percent, even accounting for the wasted materials and the other resources needed to convert the Transit Connect from a passenger to a cargo van, Ford saves thousands of dollars per van. So, the "Chicken Tax" on imports of commercial vans may reduce the number of foreign-produced vehicles in the U.S., but not by nearly as much as it would if Ford hadn't found an extremely effective, but socially costly, way around it.

Ford isn't the only company to engage in such "tariff engineering." Have you ever bought a pair of Converse sneakers? If so, you may have wondered why the soles of your new kicks are covered in a thin layer of felt. That felt wears off pretty quickly once the shoes are worn. So, why put it there in the first place? It turns out that the tariff on imported "slippers" (currently 3 percent) is much lower than the tariff on other types of imported shoes (as high as 37.5 percent). Converse has simply altered its product to resemble a slipper in order to guarantee that it pays less in import duties. That felt adds no value to consumers and actually makes the soles more slippery for a few moments until it magically disappears. But Converse has an incentive to add the felt—by reducing the import tariff it can keep the price of its sneakers lower.

Tariffs are often "sold" to the public as a patriotic gesture: "Buy American! Reserve the American market for American manufacturers!" Yet tariffs often backfire in unexpected ways. Consider what happened in 2018, when the United States imposed new tariffs on steel and aluminum. Those tariffs helped bolster the finances of American steel and aluminum producers, but they squeezed the profits of any U.S. manufacturer who used steel and aluminum to make their own product—like, for example, the most American product ever, Harley-Davidson motorcycles.

Things went downhill from there. The European Union imposed retaliatory tariffs on a variety of American-made products, including motorcycles. And so, with profits falling at home because of rising steel prices, and with retaliatory tariffs making American motorcycles very expensive (almost $2,000 more) for European buyers, Harley stunned the United States by closing some of its domestic plants (and laying off workers) and announcing that production would shift to Thailand. Ironically, the "patriotic" tariffs on American steel hurt American manufacturers of steel-using products; instead of creating jobs, it backfired and sent them to Asia.

If there's anything more American than a Harley-Davidson, it's an American farmer. Yet, a 2018 round of tariffs on Chinese goods ended up hurting the American farmer, too, when the Chinese government imposed retaliatory tariffs on imported soybeans. Soybean sales to China fell by 94 percent during 2018 as a result; family farms' bottom lines shrank. This takes us back to the "no free lunch" principle we learned in Chapter 1: To protect some American jobs from foreign competition by imposing tariffs on imported goods, we may hurt other American jobs because of the retaliatory actions of foreign governments. In effect, these policies create both winners and losers.

What might be most puzzling of all is the issue of why we worry about trade across some borders and not others. Yes, there is a movement to think more about buying locally, but we rarely see individuals railing against purchasing goods from the next town over or even across state lines. The only times we hear complaints about goods being shipped from one area to another is when we are looking at *national* borders. This begs the question: Why? Why do we only worry about competition if it is "foreign?"

The attention we pay to borders makes many Americans feel good when they do things like "buying American" or "buying local." But those good feelings come at a cost. To highlight those costs, consider a new law designed to create income security for poets, a law that requires poetry lovers to only buy poetry produced locally—no internet, no Amazon. What are the likely consequences of such a law for poetry lovers? Most are likely to find a very limited selection of very poor rhymes. (Limerick lovers might love such a law!)

But would this help poets? In most towns, there simply aren't enough poetry lovers to support even a single poet. Poets need access to a large market—a national or international market—in order to make a living through writing. Laws against imported poetry hurt both the people who produce poems and the people who read them—just like tariffs on imported goods often end up hurting both the people who consume those goods and other American producers.

It should be clear that trade benefits all who voluntarily choose to engage in it. After all, we learned in Chapter 2 that individuals weigh the expected benefits with the expected costs in making decisions. If Mack buys a car made in Japan, he must be deciding that the car is more valuable to him than the next best alternative; no one is putting a gun to his head to make him purchase this car. In addition, allowing producers with the lowest opportunity cost to make each good allows us all to get more by doing less. And that's what we really want, isn't it?

Notes

1 Bailey takes 2 hours to bake the baguette, and in the remaining 22 hours she makes 22 smoothies. Diego makes 8 smoothies. So the couple ends up with 30 smoothies and 1 baguette.
2 Bailey makes 24 smoothies; Diego uses 3 hours to make 1 baguette, and the other 21 hours to make 7 smoothies. So the couple ends up with 31 smoothies and 1 baguette.

4

NO SOUP FOR YOU

How market structure alters your choices

> *Scene: George and Jerry are at a take-out restaurant that sells the best soup in the city. But the proprietor is a bit quirky—he wants his customers to follow strict protocols when they order. George knows the rules and successfully orders. But when it's time to pay, he realizes he didn't get any bread. He asks for some, and the owner tells George he can have bread for $2. George is astounded! Everyone before him got free bread. He complains. The proprietor grows angry, and raises the price of bread to $3! George is beside himself. When he starts to object, the proprietor tells his cashier to refund George's money and take back his soup. No soup for George!*

Poor George. He just wants soup. And, bless his heart, he wants to be treated like everyone else. They got bread for free—why shouldn't he? But the seller of the soup (not so affectionately known as the "Soup Nazi") has a monopoly on the sale of his divine soups. No one else has his recipes; no one else cooks soup that will make your knees buckle.

In Chapter 3, we talked about how voluntary transactions create gains for both buyers and sellers. But sometimes, the sizes of those gains and how they are distributed between the buyer and the seller depends on what economists call the market structure—the extent of competition in the market for a particular good or service.

Businesses, of course, compete with one another in many ways—they try to offer better prices, higher quality, or more features, for example. (After all, we learned in Chapter 2 that the consumer is king!) But, the extent of this competition between firms is more than just a binary "It's competitive or it's not." Rather, firms' competitiveness spans a broad spectrum from very competitive to not competitive at all. One good rule of thumb for analyzing competition is to see how many firms there are competing for consumers' business. If there are lots of firms selling products that are nearly identical in function, quality, and features, that industry is competitive. If, on the other hand, there is only a single firm serving the entire market, economists say that a monopoly exists. Of course, many industries fall somewhere in between, so economists measure competitiveness by examining the number of producers in the industry and the degree of power that individual sellers have to raise prices.

A competitive industry is generally regarded as the best possible market structure; it's the gold standard, a benchmark that all others are compared to. In a highly competitive industry, competing firms all offer products that consumers regard as fundamentally identical—like, for example, grade A large eggs. It's really hard, if you are an egg farmer, to convince a buyer that your eggs are better than the eggs produced on the next farm over. So producers are unable to compete with each other by bragging about their product's quality or features; they must compete with one another by offering the best possible price. As a result, consumers end up receiving the lowest possible price that still allows firms to cover their costs of production. That means little profit for sellers, but lots of happy buyers.

But what happens when an industry has only one seller? Monopoly power has a couple of important implications for consumers. First, the gains from exchange are distributed differently between buyers and sellers—the buyers get a smaller share of the gains; the seller gets a larger share, a share that shows up in a fat bottom line. This is because, with nowhere else to turn, consumers find themselves at the mercy of the monopolist. And monopolists generally show no mercy—they charge the highest and most profitable price the market will bear. Second, because a monopolist charges higher prices than would exist if there were other firms competing for buyers' business, fewer people end up purchasing the monopolist's product. Instead, some buyers take their dollars elsewhere, and end up buying a "second-best" product that doesn't bring them as much happiness. As a result, the sum total of happiness in the world declines.

We see both of these effects in "The Soup Nazi," who uses his monopoly in producing knee-buckling soups to extract a very high price from his customers—a price that they pay in jumping through arbitrary hoops and suffering verbal abuse. Kramer understands the Soup Nazi: He demands perfection from himself, so he wants the same from his customers. And if they fail to live up to his expectations? No soup for them! In other words, some people who really want delicious soup have to settle for a second-best soup (or, heaven forbid, kale salad) from another seller instead. The economic pie shrinks.

Having monopoly power is a great thing for a monopolist—it allows him to earn higher profits than he would if he had to compete. So how do you become one? One way is to sew up control of a natural resource. This was the strategy employed by Cecil Rhodes and the DeBeers diamond cartel, who bought or signed long-term leases on vast swaths of the land in southern Africa where rough diamonds could be found. At one point in time, DeBeers controlled 85 percent of the world's diamond market.

Sometimes, a monopoly arises out of sheer luck—a business firm introduces the right product at the right time and manages to corner the market. This is especially likely to happen with a special type of good called a network good. Network goods are goods that become more useful when more people own them. The telephone is a network good: If only two people own phones, they can only call each other. But if a thousand people have phones, there are 499,500 different pairs of people who can call one another, which makes owning a phone much more useful. Contrast this type of good to a hamburger, which brings a hungry diner equal satisfaction whether nobody else is eating one, or everybody else is.

You might have felt the power a network good confers on a monopolist if you've ever used Facebook. Many people find themselves frustrated with Facebook—too many ads; too many concerns about security; too few posts from friends and too much sponsored content; too much creepiness when words uttered in casual conversation show up as ads in the news feed. Yet few people stand to gain by switching to a different social media platform. "I've gotta stick with Facebook—that's where all my friends are."

A third way to acquire monopoly power is to get the government to give you the exclusive right to sell a product. This tool, called exclusive franchise, has been used for thousands of years by kings and dictators as a means of enriching family, friends, and political allies. Of course, our government does the same thing—it gives inventors of innovative new products the exclusive right to sell their inventions and calls those exclusive rights a patent.

Why would the government do such a thing, if it knows that patents create monopoly power? Suppose that an enterprising young inventor labors in her garage weekends and evenings to invent something truly spectacular, like a time machine. Without a patent system that protects her right to be the sole producer of her machine, the first person who buys one can take it apart, see how it works, and then make his own version and offer a competing model.

Wouldn't that be lovely? It would bring prices down rapidly; consumers would rejoice! Except that few inventors would ever be willing to work nights and weekends to create brilliant products that can be instantly ripped off by competitors who didn't have to do the heavy lifting of research and development. Therefore, the government faces a trade-off between the availability of time machines with temporarily high prices (patents usually last about 20 years) or no time travel at all.

Of course, there are other ways to acquire monopoly power. Drug gangs often try to seize control of a market at the point of a gun (or many guns). And sometimes, businesses competing with one another can stop competing and try to behave like a monopolist—perhaps by agreeing to increase prices and not undercut one another. These tactics, by the way, are against the law—attempting to create a monopoly might land you an all-expense-paid vacation to Leavenworth Prison.

A potentially legal way for firms to stop competing is by merging operations and becoming one firm. Of course, this isn't always easy to do for both legal and operational reasons. For example, when firms in the U.S. want to merge, they must first secure permission from both the Federal Trade Commission (FTC) and the Antitrust Division of the Department of Justice. In general, the FTC and the Justice Department work to ensure that the merger does not create a large amount of monopoly power within the new firm.

Too much monopoly power has implications for product quality. Having a monopoly allows the Soup Nazi to treat his customers pretty badly without repercussion. Not all restaurants have this option, of course. If a restaurant becomes known for providing bad service, it generally loses customers and may eventually go out of business. But a monopolist is insulated from this type of competition because there is no other restaurant where one can get the monopolist's product. Consider the U.S. Postal Service. It has a constitutional monopoly on the delivery of first class mail and faces no competition. In fact, Jerry's neighbor Newman (let's say it all together: "*Hello, Newman!*") works for the Postal Service as a mail carrier.

> *Scene: Newman wants a transfer to Hawaii, and Jerry will do whatever it takes to get him one. Behind on his route, Newman convinces Jerry to help deliver mail. But then calamity strikes: Newman's supervisor calls. He knows Newman hasn't been doing his own route—too many customers have been receiving their mail. Newman has cracked the fabled 50-percent barrier! Transfer denied.*

Newman never put forth his best effort to deliver mail because he didn't have to. His customers couldn't choose another company to deliver their first-class mail, because none exists. If other carriers such as UPS or FedEx were allowed to carry first-class mail, the Postal Service would be forced to make improvements in its customer service or be left behind. This is why no postal carrier had ever surpassed the 50 percent barrier. Like the Soup Nazi, there is no reason to treat your customers well if you're the only game in town.

Also keep in mind that, regardless of how you obtain your monopoly, your high profits won't last if you can't keep new competitors from appearing. The Soup Nazi keeps the gourmet soup market to himself by having a set of recipes that are both delicious and secret. But due to a stroke of luck, Elaine discovers the Soup Nazi's secret recipes. Having been humiliated by him, she proudly proclaims that she'll share the recipes and knock him out of business. That competition breaks the Soup Nazi's monopoly; he wilts in resignation. No more soup for him!

So, we know that monopolists serve fewer people and charge them higher prices, all in the interest of increasing profits. Is there a way a monopolist can earn even *higher* profits? Yes! What if, instead of charging everyone the same, high price, our monopolist charged everyone a different price, one that was linked to each person's ability and willingness to pay? That would let monopolists earn large profits from people with deep pockets, while still selling to people with less willingness or ability to pay. Economists call this practice *price discrimination*, and it can be a great way to increase profits. We see price discrimination when the Soup Nazi charges George $3 for bread when everyone else gets their bread for free. He believes that George really wants some bread—why else would he take the chance of angering the Soup Nazi and ending up with no soup or bread at all?

There are many masterful price discriminators, but few can match movie theaters' expertise. In fact, theaters are so good at extracting dollars from their customers' wallets that economist Richard Mackenzie has devoted a book to the subject: *Why Popcorn Costs So Much at the Movies*. The biggest hurdle a price discriminator faces is being able to sort consumers into those "willing to pay a lot" and those "pretty sensitive to price." Movie theaters are so good at price discriminating that they sometimes actually get their customers to volunteer this information!

One way that movie theaters do this is by charging low prices for showings during the morning or afternoon (when the people likely to be able to pay more for a movie are at work or when folks are less likely to be on a hot date), and higher prices at night. Second, movie theaters charge students and senior citizens (both of whom are likely to be able to pay less than those of working age) a lower price by offering them a discount ... and both groups voluntarily show their IDs to qualify! Movie theaters also price discriminate by charging lower prices during the week than on weekends (when people with jobs are more likely to have free time), and by charging higher prices for new releases—people who really want to see a movie badly (and who are willing to pay more) go on opening weekend; more price-sensitive moviegoers may see the movie weeks later at the second-run theater, and the most price-sensitive customers might wait for a movie to show up in Redbox or even on Netflix. (Book publishers discriminate between readers in the same way—eager readers pay $30 for a hardback that price-sensitive readers will pay $8.95 for in paperback a year later.)

To top it all off, movie theaters leverage their monopoly power over the ability to show certain films into a monopoly on the refreshments served during those showings. This is made apparent in "The Maestro:"

> *Scene: Kramer needs help! He tried to sneak a cup of hot coffee into the movies, and burned himself badly when his concealed cup spilled. Now he wants to sue, and turns to attorney Jackie Chiles for help. Chiles asks how this unfortunate event happened, and Kramer replies that he had no choice but to sneak his coffee in—the theater doesn't allow customers to bring in outside beverages. Kramer is worried this might pose a problem, but Chiles bombastically assures him that this egregious policy violates Kramer's rights both as a consumer and as a human being.*

Policies like these create monopoly power for the theater. Unless you're willing to pull a Kramer and sneak food into the movies, you are stuck purchasing your snacks from the theater. This allows the theater to charge high prices for their sodas, popcorn, and candy—you have no other option except to go hungry!

So monopoly power can be used to raise prices and ratchet up profits. But what happens if you don't have a monopoly? It turns out that even industries with a few competing sellers can exploit the same advantages a monopolist can. One of the ways a seller in such an industry can create some monopoly power is by fostering brand loyalty. This is evident in "The Barber:"

> *Scene: Jerry and Elaine are sitting in Monk's Diner when Kramer enters. His hair, usually a mess, is calm and controlled—he's gotten one heck of a haircut! Jerry's a bit jealous—his own hair doesn't look as good. He asks Kramer who cut his hair—maybe*

> he'll give him a try. Kramer tells him that he hired Gino, the nephew of Jerry's own barber, Enzo. When Kramer refers to Enzo as "butcher," Jerry tells him he wants to switch barbers, but he can't: He's been going to Enzo for a dozen years, and if he switched, he'd hurt Enzo's feelings. Elaine needs Jerry looking his best for a bachelor auction she's sponsoring. Pointing out that Jerry never gets a good haircut, she suggests that Jerry cheat on Enzo and go to Gino instead.

Jerry is loyal to Enzo; this gives Enzo a great deal of power to exploit that emotional tie—by giving horrible haircuts, or perhaps by charging Jerry too much. Consider the American tobacco industry, an industry dominated by a few big sellers. One of the iconic cigarette brands is Camel, which used to advertise its products with the following tagline: "I'd walk a mile for a Camel." That's brand loyalty, a brand loyalty that Camel can exploit. After all, if you'd walk a mile to buy a particular brand, you'd probably pay a bit more, too.

There is another type of market where we see firms exercising monopoly power over prices, even when there are many firms producing a similar product. Economists call this monopolistic competition. In this market, there are many sellers of a product, but each produces its own version. It can vary by shape, size, color, or location. Some are popular with consumers (leading to market power), while others are not. Location is a big issue, as can be seen in Seinfeld's monologue for "The Café:"

> Scene: Jerry is at a comedy club performing. He's talking about the turnover we see in particular store locations. One day it's one type of store; the next day it's something else. Jerry suggests these locations are some type of Bermuda triangle, and we really will never understand why businesses fail there over and over again.

Think about gas stations and convenience marts. Why do some places thrive while others close? Choosing the right corner really seems to matter. Perhaps drivers prefer right turns, or the lighting is better in one place than another. Location is just one dimension a firm can use to distinguish itself from others.

Now, consider fast food hamburgers. They are all similar, yes, but a little different as well. And firms who produce these burgers spend millions of dollars on advertising to convince you that their version is the one that is best. It may be flame-broiled, grass-fed beef, on a soft bun with just the right condiments. If they succeed in convincing you that their version is best, you may just be willing to pay a bit more for their burger. That gives them some monopoly power even though they do not stand alone in their market. Of course, they are *somewhat* limited in what they can charge. Very few customers would be willing to pay $20 for a Whopper, even if they are convinced it's the best fast food hamburger in the world! There are just too many other close substitutes.

And that is really the key to understanding market structures. How many substitutes are there and how closely do they resemble one another? The more substitutes there are, and the more identical the product, the more competitive the market. The more competitive the market, the greater the gains from trade to consumers, leaving producers with little profit. However, if you are the single seller of a unique product, you've got tremendous market power and can earn much greater profits while delivering a lower-quality product. You've got made in the shade, baby!

5

LOW FLOW? I DON'T LIKE THE SOUND OF THAT

Interference in the market

> Scene: Jerry's apartment. Kramer enters, and informs Jerry that the building superintendent is busy changing all of the apartments' shower heads. Jerry replies that the super's going to do his next. He tells Kramer that the new shower heads are all low flow. Kramer, disconcerted, tells Jerry that he doesn't like the way that sounds.

In previous chapters, we discussed the reasons why the free exchange of goods and services that takes place in markets creates wealth for society. But at times, both the government and cultural tradition intervene in the market in ways that impede free exchange. We already discussed one of the ways in which the government does this in Chapter 3, when we looked at the effects of tariffs on international trade. This chapter discusses the effects of other types of interventions in markets.

In "The Shower Head," the government intervention takes the form of a legal restriction on how much water a shower head should allow to flow. Does that sound like a silly law? Well, maybe, but such a law was passed at the federal level just a few years before "The Shower Head" aired. That federal law required all new shower heads to allow no more than 2.5 gallons of water to flow through them each minute.

One theme we will return to often in this chapter is that such interventions have direct effects, but that those interventions also have unintended consequences. "The Shower Head" makes the direct effects of the low-flow law very clear: The weak, low-pressure showers that the new heads create are horrible. Kramer relies on an invigorating shower—it's part of his essence. The new shower, which can't even rinse the shampoo out of his hair, is stealing his very Kramer-ness!

Why would the government pass such a law? On the surface, it's to stop the wasteful use of water. To economists, this seems odd—after all, people pay for the water they use in the same way they pay for the coffee they drink or the clothes they wear. And yet, we have no laws that require all pants to have 30" waists, nor do we have laws that require coffee to be sold only in eight-ounce cups.

Whatever the reasoning behind it, the law requiring low flow will most likely reduce water use. Whether this is the best way to stop the wasteful use of water is another question. Anyone who has ever flown in to Phoenix will likely understand—the city, one of the hottest and driest in the United States, sparkles emerald green and aquamarine from the air, filled as it is with golf courses and swimming pools. And truly, nothing says "the desert" like bright green lawns...

So maybe there is a better way to reduce water use. No matter—low-flow shower heads are the law of the land, and they probably do reduce water consumption. But the great 19th century economist Frederic Bastiat cautions us to "Stop there! Your theory is confined to that which is seen; it takes no account of that which is not seen." So what might be the unseen consequences of a low-flow shower head law?

To figure out those unseen consequences, let's think about how people will react to lousy shower heads. They want more water! They may even *need* more water—you gotta rinse that shampoo! So, one way to compensate for a weak, dribbly shower is simply to spend more time in the shower: That ten-minute shower becomes a 20-minute washfest. And, if one shower head limits you to 2.5 gallons per minute, people thirsty for more H_2O can double that by simply adding a *second* shower head! Indeed, if you've done any house hunting lately, you may have found that many new homes have fancy shower systems with two, three, or even four shower heads!

There's another way that people faced with a low-flow law can get more water when they're renovating their bathrooms: They can buy a used shower head, one produced before the restriction became law. So, one unintended consequence of the low-flow law is that it creates a new market in used shower heads, with thousands of contractors and middlemen scouring Habitat ReStores for precious pre-ban shower heads.

But what if there aren't enough pre-ban shower heads available? One way to lay your paws on a high-flow shower head is to smuggle one in from abroad. In "The Shower Head," Newman draws on a shifty, unnamed connection to source a supply of black-market shower heads. He tells Jerry that they're being smuggled in from Yugoslavia, where people are fanatical about their showers. Jerry, skeptical, tells him that from what he's seen, he's not so sure. Nevertheless, he and Kramer both agree to give the black-market shower heads a try.

Kramer and Newman meet the seller in a dark alley and each buys a shower head out of his van. This isn't, of course, their preferred place to shop—they would rather be able to walk into a local hardware store to buy what they need. But the only shower heads available at the store are those with low flow. So Kramer and Newman must bear the additional cost of finding a black-market seller and meeting him in a secluded place to engage, at the risk of fines or imprisonment, in a trade that will make them better off. A government law designed to get people to use less water has turned ordinary citizens into common criminals! (Meanwhile, two blocks away, people are lined up around the block at the car wash...)

Scene: Elaine is in dire straits. Her favorite birth control method, the spermicidal sponge, has been taken off the market by the government. Elaine responds by scouring the neighborhood for any remaining stock, searching pharmacies and grocery stores for miles in every direction. George can't believe she's going to so much trouble, but Elaine assures him that it's worth it; she's loyal to her sponge.

Eventually, Elaine locates a stash of sponges at a pharmacy, and purchases the last case. Knowing that she'll never be able to locate another, Elaine has to economize in a way she's never had to before. The regulation reduces Elaine's happiness: She forgoes having sex with her current boyfriend, because she's just not sure he is sponge-worthy. A confused Jerry points out that Elaine likes her boyfriend, and that, after all, that's what the sponge is for. But Elaine has done the cost–benefit analysis and knows that her sponges are now more scarce. She tells Jerry that with the sponge now off the market, she'll have to be more careful how she uses her stash. She can't afford to waste a single sponge.

Note how this relates to our discussion about scarcity and opportunity cost from Chapter 1. The sponge is now more scarce, and the opportunity cost of using one is much higher. This is why Elaine has to reconsider her decision of who is "sponge-worthy" and who is not. This is a real problem—if you use a sponge today, you lose the opportunity to use that sponge later should a better ... candidate ... come along. And you can't just pop down to the local drug store to get another; they are no longer available. Figuring out whether someone is "sponge-worthy" or not is such a difficult problem that economist Avinash Dixit had to use calculus in order to solve it; his solution was published in a peer-reviewed economics journal.[1]

The government often finds itself trying to protect its citizenry from all kinds of evils. Sometimes, it even tries to protect citizens from themselves. Safety regulations are a good example. Sometimes safety regulations do good things for consumers: There's a reason you want your electrician to follow a standard code; if your electrician cuts corners, you might find yourself unexpectedly warm. But sometimes safety regulations may over-reach (at least in some people's opinions): Mandatory seatbelt laws protect drivers from their own reckless driving. And, like all policies, there may be unintended consequences, as we discussed in Chapter 2.

For example, mandatory seatbelt laws may make drivers feel safer, leading them to drive more recklessly. That puts nearby pedestrians and cyclists at risk: In the 20 months after Britain established a law requiring front-seat car passengers to wear seatbelts, 77 more pedestrians were killed in traffic accidents than were killed in the 20 months prior to the law. An additional 63 bicyclists were killed as well.

Many states have laws restricting restaurants from selling rare or medium-rare hamburgers. Why? If meat grinders are not properly cleaned and maintained, ground beef may possibly contain harmful bacteria that will not die off unless the burger reaches an internal temperature of 155 degrees for more than 15 seconds. Of course, this disappoints customers who prefer their burgers a little on the pinker side. If such eaters know and willingly accept the risks of consuming undercooked ground beef, why should the government prohibit this exchange from taking place?

Another example is cheese made from non-pasteurized milk. The FDA restricts the sale of such cheeses across state lines (unless aged 60 days or more) and prohibits people from importing them from abroad. This prevents Americans from enjoying lots of tasty cheeses, but it also prevents them from enjoying listeria, salmonella, and E. coli too.

Sometimes, of course, the government passes regulations in the name of safety that don't actually do anything to make anyone safer! In Louisiana, you must pass a state licensing exam if you want to arrange flowers. In past years, that exam has been so difficult to pass that fewer than half of those taking the exam succeed. Former Louisiana agriculture commissioner Bob Odom justified the licensing requirement because of a "need to protect consumers." Yet no one we've ever asked, in states without such licensing requirements, has ever been harmed by an errant bouquet. In fact, the marketplace is more than capable of solving this problem: Give me a crappy floral arrangement, I'll never visit your establishment again … and I'll put pictures of it all over Facebook and Instagram to make sure that none of my friends do, either!

The real motivation for the exam becomes apparent when we learn that the vexing hands-on portion of the exam was graded by previously licensed florists. Remember what we said in Chapter 2 about incentives? If you were a licensed florist in Louisiana, would you want to give a high grade to a test-taker who threatened your livelihood? The Louisiana florist licensing exam is simply a way for the government to confer a special economic advantage on previously licensed florists!

Governments can attempt to regulate prices in markets as well. For example, many local governments attempt to help the poor by limiting the price that landlords can charge for apartments. In economics, this is called a "price ceiling," which is a maximum price that can legally be charged for something. The goal of a price ceiling on rent is to ensure that low-income individuals have access to safe, affordable housing. This policy, of course, has good intentions. But is that what actually happens?

> *Scene: Jerry comes into his apartment after talking with his building superintendents, Harold and Manny. He tells Elaine that his upstairs neighbor, Mrs. Hudwalker, has died, and that he's managed to secure the apartment for Elaine. Elaine is simply giddy to hear this. Then Jerry tells her the rent is only $400, and simply giddy turns to positively ecstatic. She tells Jerry how happy she'll be to be living there, in the same building with her best friend. She can't wait, she tells him—she'll be at his place all the time!*

Elaine is elated for two reasons—she gets to live closer to Jerry and she will be getting a very nice apartment for only $400 per month. What a deal! Keep in mind that Elaine is not exactly poor. In fact, in most places with rent control, there is no limit on who can live there. All she has to do is be the next in line. And believe us, there will be a line. Because the problem with placing a ceiling on the amount of rent that can be charged is that it will lead to a shortage of clean, safe apartments. Building owners may choose to turn the apartments into condominiums and sell them outright to individuals rather than rent them at below-market prices. Or, if they continue to rent them out, they may stop maintaining the building. There will be no new paint and carpeting when a tenant leaves, no bright lighting in the hallways. So, the supply of nice apartments will dwindle. But just as fewer apartments are being offered for rent, more people are trying to find them. Lured by attractive rents, people who may have shared an apartment with a roommate to split expenses now try to find their own place. Kids (finally!) start trying to move out of their parents' basements and live on their own. With more people looking for fewer apartments, shortages result.

In markets without restrictions, goods and services get distributed to those willing and able to pay the most. But, in the case of a price ceiling, this does not occur. Instead, goods and services get rationed in some other way—most likely on a "first-come first-served" basis. This means that Elaine can get the rent-controlled apartment by simply being the first to talk with the building superintendent about it.

Of course, we know (from Chapter 2) that people respond to incentives. The landlord has something that many people want. Perhaps there is a way he can make some extra money from this situation. This may lead to a black market where goods and services are exchanged under the table. This is exactly what occurs in "The Apartment." Elaine doesn't end up with the apartment after all because another individual offers the building superintendents $5,000 to move him to the front of the line. While this practice is illegal, it often occurs when shortages exist. In rent-controlled New York City, this is such a common practice that the bribes have entered the vernacular as "key money:" "I'd love to rent you this apartment, but I'll need to cut a new key. That'll be $5,000." And, because the apartment ends up going to the person who is willing to pay the most, economists would argue that this moves the market back to an efficient outcome.

Recall, however, that the goal of rent control is to help ensure lower-income individuals a supply of affordable housing. It's true that rent controls help keep monthly rents affordable. But by creating a shortage of available apartments, rent control makes it harder for the poor to find housing—after all, with ten applicants for every apartment, a landlord would be foolish to offer a unit to the applicant with the lowest income. And the informal institutionalization of key money makes it harder for the poor to move—lots of lower-income families can likely afford a $600 monthly rent payment, but few can come up with $10,000 key money all in one shot. So, by making it harder to find an apartment, and harder to get into an apartment, rent control likely makes it harder, not easier, for the poor to find decent housing at a reasonable price.

There are other laws and social customs that result in a less-than-ideal use of scarce resources, too. Elaine points this out in "The Chinese Restaurant," when she laments having to stand in line for a table. What kind of horrible custom is it to seat people on a first-come, first-served basis, she wonders. Why aren't people seated in order of who's hungriest? Elaine has a point, which is why some individuals may slip the maître d' some cash to get a table more quickly. Or, perhaps a person can pay someone to take their place in line or even hire a stand-in. In fact, a new profession has been born—professional line waiters! There's a business in Washington, D.C. that charges $30 per hour to be a stand-in, not a bad deal for those with a high opportunity cost of time. This kind of service, like the institution of key money, can result in a more efficient outcome, even if it doesn't seem exactly fair to those standing in line for themselves.

We see human beings' ability to produce efficient outcomes in spite of laws and social custom in other markets as well. That sold out Lady Gaga concert? Those first in line for tickets may then resell them for a price much higher than face value. This practice, known as scalping, used to be illegal in most U.S. states. In "The Opera," Kramer and George have two extra tickets for the opening night of "Pagliacci" (starring the late, great tenor Luciano Pavarotti), and they attempt to scalp them outside the theater. While they know this practice is illegal, the lure of making some extra cash convinces them to ignore the law. The prospect of scalping opening night tickets for Pavarotti turns George into a self-professed opera lover!

Scalping is now legal in most states, and ticket resellers have become all the rage. StubHub is a popular website for reselling tickets to almost any event. Ticketmaster, the firm that manages original ticket sales for events across the U.S., owns its own reseller as well. These resellers put the tickets in the hands of those who value them the most. Therefore, making scalping legal has improved the market's efficiency. Individuals may not get to see every concert they want to, but more than likely that is because they aren't willing to pay a high enough price for a ticket rather than because the ticket isn't available.

Of course, it's not always governments that think the market somehow "gets it wrong" and feels compelled to intervene. Sometimes, private actors (no, not the Brad Pitt kind) feel the same urge. Consider ice cream: In the 1990s, Ben and Jerry's (who practice "Caring Capitalism") capped the salary of their CEO, limiting it to five times the salary of the lowest-paid employee. When CEO Ben Cohen retired, that salary (about $80,000) wasn't high enough to attract any qualified applicants. Ben and Jerry's increased the ratio to seven to one, but even that proved ineffective at attracting and retaining a qualified candidate. By 2000, the cap had been raised again, to 17 to one (about $500,000); it was abandoned shortly thereafter when Ben and Jerry's was acquired by Dutch conglomerate Unilever.

Ben and Jerry's repeated attempts to establish a meaningful cap on CEO pay were undoubtedly motivated by a sense of fairness. But Ben and Jerry failed to realize that no matter how much they disliked the price the market had set for a talented CEO, the market got it right: A good CEO costs what a good CEO costs, no matter how much one might wish it were otherwise.

Sometimes the market sets a price higher than fair-minded individuals might like; sometimes the market sets it lower. Consider coffee. I mean, who doesn't love a little caffeine in the morning, right? And who among us hasn't winced a time or two after forking over $8 for an early morning grande half-caf skinny soy latte? All that money, and yet the poor farmer who grew our designer coffee beans receives so little. Wouldn't it be nice if Starbucks saw a little less of that money, and the coffee farmer a bit more?

And so, to correct for the fact that the market *appears* to have underpriced the primary ingredient in our cafe au lait, benevolent organizations spring up like flowers after a desert rain to certify certain brands of coffee as "fair trade" coffee— coffee in which the coffee grower receives an above-market price for the beans.

Here's the good thing about fair trade coffee: Consumers who want to alleviate their guilt over the economic plight of the coffee farmer can buy fair trade coffee at what is often a premium price, and drink it with a clear conscience.

But, fundamentally, the reason coffee beans are so cheap is *because there's too much coffee*. And remember one of the key principles developed in Chapter 2: People respond to incentives. One of the big incentives fair-trade coffee creates is the incentive for coffee growers, now receiving a premium price, to plant even more … *which puts more downward pressure on the price of coffee*. As a result, the organizations that certify coffee as fair-trade often have to limit either who will be allowed to join the favored farmers who receive the fair-trade price, or attempt to limit the amount they produce. And yet, even with those limits, there is not enough demand for fair-trade coffee to absorb all of the coffee certified as fair trade; generally, only one-third to one-half of that coffee can be sold at fair-trade prices. The rest is often sold as ordinary coffee, where it *pushes down the price every other coffee farmer receives for his crop*. We can feel bad about this, and we can try to invent ways to make our coffee growers happier. But there are probably better ways to improve the welfare of coffee growers than offering them artificially high prices that encourage them to produce more … because, remember, low coffee prices are ultimately caused by *too much coffee*. What a vicious cycle is started by those who think they know better than the market does what something is worth.

The point is that there is a great deal of information in markets. The demand for a product is based on individuals' value of the good (along with their ability to pay for it). The supply is affected by the cost of the resources used to produce the good (which, remember, are scarce). The interaction of these forces creates the market price of the good; this price reflects both the good's value to consumers and its cost of production. No entity (the government or do-gooders) knows better than the market what these values are, and setting prices at any level other than the market price will likely make a society worse off rather than better off. So repeat now after us, "In markets we trust!"

Note

1 See Dixit, A. (2012). An option value problem from *Seinfeld. Economic Inquiry, 50*(2), 563–565.

6

MY RODS AND CONES ARE ALL SCREWED UP!

Living with externalities

Scene: A new Kenny Rogers Roasters chicken restaurant has opened across the street from Kramer's apartment, and its neon sign is just outside Kramer's window. The bright red chicken-shaped light is making Kramer even more crazy than usual—he can't sleep worth a darn. He's helping himself to a bowl of Jerry's cereal when Jerry notices something amiss. Instead of milk, Kramer is adding tomato juice! Kramer takes a big bite and spits it out. He tells Jerry that the tomato juice looked like milk to him. That big red Kenny Rogers sign has ruined his vision; his "rods and cones" are all messed up!

The previous chapter discussed instances when interference with a well-functioning private market creates adverse consequences. But there are times when private markets don't function so well—when the costs and benefits of transactions aren't completely captured by the buyer and seller. In those cases, markets tend to produce "wrong" quantities of the goods and services—either more than we might want, or, sometimes, less. This chapter discusses different instances in which markets "get it wrong," in that they fail to provide the ideal amount of a good or service to society.

One case in which this happens is when the act of producing an item for sale imposes costs on someone who is not involved in the transaction. To understand this, consider someone who hires an accountant to do her taxes. This transaction doesn't affect anyone but the taxpayer and her accountant. The person next door is probably completely unaware that these two individuals have struck a deal with one another. In this case, taxpayers and accountants who make cost–benefit decisions (to hire or not to hire, to agree to do someone else's taxes or not) also end up making decisions that are good for society.

Contrast that with someone who sets up a barbeque pit in his backyard in order to sell racks of ribs in the neighborhood. When someone asks the pitmaster to cook another rack of ribs, the smoke the pitmaster generates might bother his next-door neighbor. And if the cost of that bother is high enough (maybe it irritates the neighbor's asthma, or maybe it sends the neighbor's Rottweiler into an annoying drooling and barking frenzy), what looks like a great decision for the pitmaster and his customer might turn out to be a poor decision for society.

The key to understanding this paradox lies in the nature of costs. The pitmaster faces what we call "private costs" that include things like the cost of the meat, the charcoal, and the opportunity cost of the time needed to smoke the ribs. But the act of smoking the ribs also includes "external costs" that are borne by the pitmaster's neighbor. Those costs (often referred to as a "negative externality") are real; it's just that the pitmaster doesn't have to pay them. And because the pitmaster doesn't have to pay them, he may make decisions that are in his own interest, but not in the best interest of society. For example, if the pitmaster's private costs are $10, and his customer values the ribs at $12, the pitmaster will agree to sell the customer ribs and potentially earn a $2 profit. But if the act of making those ribs imposes $5 worth of damage on the pitmaster's next-door neighbor, the true cost of making the ribs (often referred to as the "social cost") is $15. This means that every time the pitmaster makes a slab of ribs, he gets richer by $2, but society gets $3 poorer, having spent $15 to make $12 worth of ribs. Our pitmaster is simply making too many ribs.

Consider this chapter's opening scene from "The Chicken Roaster." Poor Kramer! He's the classic victim of a negative externality. Kenny and his customers are buying and selling succulent wings and thighs; Kramer bears some of the cost in lost sleep and mixed up rods and cones. That's not fair—why does society let things like this happen!?

Well, society might actually *want* this to happen, because it's possible that the gains enjoyed by Kenny and his customers more than outweigh the costs imposed on Kramer. To help explain why, let's return to the barbeque for a minute: Suppose that a second pitmaster lives around the corner, and her private cost of making ribs is only $6. Then, even when she forces her neighbor to bear $5 worth of smoke damage for each rack roasted, she's still able to take $11 of costs (her $6 of private costs and the $5 of negative externality) and turn those costs into $12 worth of ribs. Society is a winner in this case (even though the poor neighbor is a loser); these are ribs we *don't* want to get rid of.

And even Kramer doesn't want to get rid of Kenny Rogers Roasters! When Jerry threatens to run Kenny Rogers out of business, Kramer protests. He hates the light, but he *loves* the chicken. He loves it so much, in fact, that Jerry accuses Kramer of having a little problem. Not true, says Kramer: It's a *big* problem!

As we mentioned in Chapter 2, rational individuals make decisions by weighing the costs and benefits of an action. For Kramer, the benefits of the chicken outweigh the costs. To satisfy his appetite for chicken, Kramer tolerates the light. He'd rather have the chicken and the red blinking light than not have chicken at all, even if it does mess up his rods and cones.

In other words, we don't want to eliminate all pollution, because often we enjoy the things that created the pollution so much that we're willing to put up with the collateral damage. This is why even hardened environmentalists drive polluting cars—they know they're imposing costs on other people, but getting from Point A (where a beached whale has just been pushed back into the ocean) to Point B (where a new housing development has just been shelved in order to preserve the habitat of an endangered newt) is so valuable that they're willing to do it.

The truth is, the world is *full* of negative externalities; it would be practically impossible to eliminate them all. Consider this, from "The Smelly Car:"

> *Scene: Jerry and Elaine have just picked up his car from the valet at a restaurant. But something's wrong—his car smells horrible! Elaine smells it, too, and pronounces it worse than any half-dozen horrible smells Jerry might name. What is this awful stench? It's B.O.! And it must have come from the valet. Jerry really wants to get the smell out. He takes it to a car wash, but they want him to pay hundreds of dollars to de-stench his ride. He doesn't feel he should be responsible for this cost and demands the restaurant pay for his car to be cleaned.*

A world without B.O. might be good for our noses, but eliminating that particular negative externality comes at a great cost—just ask anyone who's ever been in the locker room after a high school basketball game. While the people at Axe might salivate at the potential profits such a world would create, the costs (no more basketball games or gardening, and mandatory hourly showers for the particularly odoriferous) would likely be too high.

We've been using various forms of pollution (light, smoke, and odor) to illustrate the notion of negative externalities. It's worth noting that there are other kinds, too. Consider the episode "The Good Samaritan," where Kramer begins unexpectedly going into seizures because of *Entertainment Tonight* host Mary Hart's voice. That plot line was based on a real-life case from 1991 that was actually documented in the *New England Journal of Medicine*.

You might not go into convulsions at the sound of Mary Hart's voice, but that doesn't mean negative externalities don't affect you. Consider this little project, for example: Type your home address into your state's sex offender registry and see what pops up. You know who *doesn't* want to do this, ignorance being bliss? Parents of young children. But you know who *does*? Potential homebuyers. And they do, often enough that the presence of a sex offender in the neighborhood shows up in housing prices: If you're interested in selling your house, having a sex offender in the neighborhood will reduce the amount you receive by about 6 percent; having one next door will reduce your home's market value by 12 percent. That's a negative externality!

And there are others, too:

- Texting while driving dramatically increases the risk to innocent pedestrians.
- In states where marijuana production is legal, people living near pot farms complain of a horrible smell.
- Your decision to take the freeway to work instead of surface streets slows thousands of other cars down by just the tiniest amount; the combined decisions of thousands of commuters often brings city traffic to a standstill.

- Use of antibiotics encourages the proliferation of drug-resistant bacteria; using antibiotics today may reduce their effectiveness for everyone in the future.
- Breathing creates carbon dioxide, which contributes to global warming.

Is there a silver lining in this cloud of negative externalities? Yes! Because sometimes, instead of imposing *costs* on innocent bystanders, market activities create *benefits* for those bystanders! After all, who doesn't enjoy walking by a bakery—even if you're gluten intolerant, the smell of freshly baked bread is, well, the greatest thing since sliced bread!

One huge positive externality that we all benefit from is the external benefit created by vaccinations. When you get your flu shot, you are less likely to get sick, and you're also less likely to give the flu to anyone around you. You suffer the discomfort of the immunization, and your spouse and kids share in the benefits. This secondhand immunity, often referred to as herd immunity, is exceedingly valuable for people too weak to tolerate a vaccine—often, the very young, or those with compromised immune systems. This is why it's so important for healthy people to get their shots. Because when they don't, you get outbreaks of totally preventable yet often deadly diseases like measles, mumps, and whooping cough.

One product that is often credited with creating a positive externality is education. When we make a child attend school, we increase the likelihood that the child will have the knowledge and skills to develop things that everyone else will get to enjoy the benefits of: The next iPhone, the next hit musical, the "Mansierre," or a solution to global warming. The student does the hard work; the rest of society shares in the benefits of that work.

So positive externalities are dandy things. Unfortunately, when positive externalities exist, the producers of the good that creates the externality often tend to make less of that good than is ideal. To illustrate, consider a beekeeper, who manages hives that produce the honey she sells. The beekeeper enjoys the private benefits of having a hive—she gets to sell honey. And so, she decides each year how many hives she can successfully manage in order to make the most profit possible.

But bees create a positive externality—they pollinate crops in nearby fields! Let's suppose that each hive produces $500 extra in yields for farmers. Those farmers get that $500 gift for free, but if the beekeeper had some way to get them to kick a bit of that money back to her, she might keep even more hives that would create more profit for her and which would pollinate even more crops (and increase the profits for farmers as well)!

So, if society tends to have too many goods that create negative externalities, and too few goods that produce positive externalities, is there anything we can do to get the producers to produce the ideal amounts? Yes! Remember in Chapter 5 when we told you that government interventions in the marketplace tended to make the world poorer? Well, when goods produce significant externalities, either positive or negative, government intervention actually has the potential to make the world richer rather than poorer!

Products that come with negative externalities tend to be overproduced because producers get to shift some of their costs onto innocent bystanders as collateral damage. One way to get producers to produce the ideal amount is for the government to make them pay the dollar value of that damage; that way, they consider the entire social cost of the goods they produce and not just their own private costs. The government can do this by making producers pay a tax for each unit they produce. (A tax like this is called a Pigovian tax, after economist Arthur Pigou, who invented it.)

Let's return to our two pitmasters for a minute to illustrate. Remember that each of them imposes a cost of $5 on their neighbors, but that the first one isn't very cost-efficient (his ribs are high-cost ribs that make society worse off), while the second one is more cost-efficient (her ribs are a gain for society, even when the externality is taken into account). We want our first pitmaster not to produce ribs; we want our second to continue. If the government imposes a $5 tax on each slab of ribs, the first producer will find that making ribs isn't worth his while—he'll have to pay $15 to produce ribs that he can sell for $12. The second will continue to sell, as her costs, even after the tax, are only $11, and she can sell $12 ribs at a profit. Society gets richer by weeding out the first pitmaster, the one whose ribs imposed a $3 cost on society for every rack sold. And, just as important, the policy allows the second pitmaster to still remain in business.

In a similar light, the government can subsidize products (in other words, send payments directly to producers) that produce positive externalities. If, for example, our beekeeper has trouble collecting from farmers the $500 benefit that her bees create, then a government payment of $500 for each hive ought to be a suitable substitute. The beekeeper keeps more hives; the farmers receive external benefits, and society as a whole gains.

The real issue when there is an externality present is that the property rights of some resources are ill-defined. Who owns the air around the pitmasters' and their neighbors' homes? The pitmaster who wants to make a profit? Or the neighbor who wants to breathe fresh air and not suffer from an asthma attack? When it is not clear who has which rights, everyone wants to claim them as their own.

There is no better example of ill-defined property rights than the small space between rows of seats on an airplane. As this space has gotten smaller over time, more and more conflicts have arisen over who owns this space. Suppose that Kylie and Ethan are two passengers on a flight from New York to Los Angeles. Kylie needs to get ready for an important presentation and lowers her tray table so she can set her laptop up. But then Ethan, sitting in the seat in front of her, decides he wants to recline his seat so he can be more comfortable on the long flight. Reclining the seat makes it very difficult for Kylie to have her laptop open completely and impairs her ability to work. Who is in the right in this case? Does Ethan have the right to recline? Does Kylie have the right to work? It all depends on who is entitled to the space between the rows of seats. Without a clear assignment of the right to that space, we're likely to see Kylie and Ethan both shouting, "No, it's *mine!*"

Enter the "Knee Defender." The Knee Defender is a gadget (first sold in 2003) that Kylie can attach to her tray table to prevent Ethan from reclining his seat. With this device, Kylie is able to seize the right to the disputed space. This will likely make Ethan a bit angry. In 2014, two passengers engaged in an altercation aboard a United Airlines flight from Los Angeles to Newark because a passenger had used the Knee Defender. All U.S. airlines have now banned this device, thereby assigning the property rights to the passenger who wants to recline. (Hurray for Ethan! And, as we will see a bit later, hurray for Kylie, too!)

In "The Parking Space," George finds himself in a situation involving ill-defined property rights.

> *Scene: George and Elaine need to park, and George has found an open spot right in front of Jerry's building. Pretty lucky, right? George pulls past the space and begins to back in, just as another driver (Mike) begins to pull into the same space head-first. George confronts Mike: He can't put it in head-first, that's not how it's done! Mike is miffed, too: George was so far beyond the space that it didn't look like he was going to park there. With two cars angled halfway into one space, an argument ensues. Mike honks; George honks back. When it is clear that Mike isn't going to just give up the space, a frustrated George does the only thing that comes to mind: He calls Mike a jerk.*

So, is George right? Is Mike a jerk for "stealing" his parking space? Or is Mike entitled to it? Once again, this is a situation where there is no clear answer. In fact, throughout "The Parking Space" many people (neighbors, policemen, etc.) weigh in on this very issue: Who has the right to a vacant parking spot on a public street? When property rights aren't defined, a resource will often be claimed by the first person to grab it. Individuals will scramble to be that first person, and conflict will ensue. Or, after someone lays claim to the resource, others will complain loudly, "Unfair!"

From the economist's standpoint, the real problem isn't the conflict over the resource, or that some people feel that they've received an unfair outcome. The real problem is that every resource has a best use: Kylie might value the space between the airplane seats more than Ethan; George might value the parking space more highly than Mike; residents of the L.A. basin might value breathing clean air more than factories value the ability to pollute. From society's standpoint, we want to extract the greatest benefit from every scarce resource. But when a resource doesn't belong to anyone, the first person to grab it won't necessarily be the person who can make best use of it.

How can this type of issue be resolved? If the major source of conflict is that the resource (parking space, knee space, the air above and the water below) doesn't belong to anybody, then a good first step in resolving conflict might be to assign the right to the resource to someone. Once that's done, once the resource becomes someone's property, then it's a marketable commodity that can be purchased by the person who values it most. In the case of pollution, polluters might pay victims for the right to spew smoke into the atmosphere. Or, oddly, residents might pay polluters not to pollute!

We see this in "The Stakeout:"

> *Scene: Jerry is Elaine's "plus one" at a birthday party at a piano bar. Unfortunately, the pianist isn't very good. In fact, his playing is making it difficult for Jerry to schmooze Vanessa, a beautiful woman he's just met and is intrigued by. They're trying to talk and are having a hard time hearing over the music. In a move that would impress many economists, Vanessa asks Jerry how much he thinks they would have to tip to get the pianist to close his keyboard and go home. Jerry offers to contribute $5. Vanessa offers to pass her hat around the room so others can donate to the cause, too.*

Here, Jerry and Vanessa are considering providing a tip to the piano player—not to reward him, but to bribe him to stop! This would eliminate the negative externality the piano player creates, and it would put the airspace in the hands of the people (Jerry and Vanessa) who value it most. They value silence more than the money; the piano player earns more if he *doesn't* play than he would by playing. And that outcome doesn't require any heavy-handed regulation—the simple process of negotiation creates an outcome favorable to everyone.

The same type of negotiation can help resolve other cases of conflict over resources. Consider Kylie and Ethan, for example. Suppose Kylie values the ability to work at $50 and Ethan values the ability to recline at $40. Now that the airlines have determined that Ethan has the right to recline his seat (first, by installing seats that recline and then by outlawing the Knee Defender), Kylie could negotiate with Ethan to have him transfer that right to her. Suppose she offers him $44. If Ethan accepts, Kylie gets something she values at $50 for only $44; Ethan receives $44 for something he only values at $40. Everyone wins, and the extra space goes to the person who values it most. But what if Ethan values the space at $60? Then no offer Kylie can make will be enough to convince Ethan to give up his right to recline. And this is still a great outcome—Ethan keeps the right to recline and the space gets put to its best use.

So does Kylie offer to pay Ethan to not recline his seat? In a perfect world, yes. But more often than not, Kylie would feel uncomfortable in making such an offer. It may be socially unacceptable to offer a "bribe" to someone to stop imposing an external cost on you. Economists call this a "transaction cost." It is not costless to settle the externality if it goes against social norms and we care what others think about us (and we do—probably a bit too much, but that's a lesson for another book!). Transaction costs can impede parties from solving externality problems on their own.

Transaction costs like social norms may prevent some worthwhile negotiations over resources from happening. But they won't *always* prevent people from solving externality problems on their own. Consider what happened in March 2019 at the beginning of a five-hour flight (yes, we're a little bit obsessed with airline seating). A man had just settled into his aisle seat when a very large male passenger claimed the window seat next to him. The first man complained to a flight attendant, who told the obese passenger that he would have to pay extra for a second seat.

Unfortunately, the flight had no extra seats. Rather than make the obese passenger leave the airplane and book a later flight, the first man made the following offer to the obese passenger: "Look, I'll put up with this if you give me $150—that's half the cost of this flight, and that would compensate me enough for the circumstances." The obese man agreed, a deal was struck, and $150 changed hands. When the aisle passenger told his story on Reddit, many commenters insulted him and thought that he "blackmailed" the other passenger for being obese. But economists would applaud this agreement! In an economist's eyes, the obese passenger was imposing an external cost on his seatmate. With the property right to his own seat well-defined, the aisle passenger was able to sell the right to one-third of his seat to his stockier seatmate. The larger man got to stay on the flight; the aisle passenger received sufficient compensation for the discomfort and inconvenience. Win-Win! (This may be yet another example of why economists are rarely invited to dinner parties!)

Private individuals have also crafted a meaningful solution to the problem of parking spaces. Chicago, the city of broad shoulders, is not known for its mild winters. In fact, winter can be downright brutal. And in a big city where lots of people don't have off-street parking like driveways and garages, on-street parking is often at a premium.

So what happens when a snowstorm hits? Everyone parked on the street has to dig out their car, and when they do, they leave an empty, clean, shoveled space for someone else to use. But, in Chicago, residents have crafted an informal but respected solution to the problem of "stolen" parking spots: If you shovel out a parking space in the morning before work, you can leave some lawn furniture in that space, and you're entitled to that space when you get home. This informal and extra-legal arrangement seems to work quite well; there seems to be a common understanding supporting its use. In fact, even in places where the law prohibits using lawn furniture to save parking spaces, cities seem to turn a blind eye to it. After huge blizzards in 2010, Baltimore mayor Stephanie Rawlings-Blake said the city wouldn't enforce a ban on parking chairs, saying that the practice could no more be stopped than the practice of people calling one another "Hon."

Externality problems encompass what happens when someone's actions impose indirect costs on another. But problems also arise when someone is free to enjoy the *benefits* of a resource without sharing the cost. This type of resource is called "non-excludable," meaning that individuals can't be prevented from using the item even if they haven't paid for it. Take National Public Radio (NPR). It is broadcast and anyone with a radio can listen to it. There is no subscription fee, and there aren't even any annoying commercials to listen to. Just programming. How is it funded? While it receives a tiny bit of money from the government, the majority of the programming funds comes from public donations from listeners. But wait! Didn't we just say you could listen to it for free? Yes, you can! And if you listen to NPR frequently, and you do not donate to their funding drives, economists may call you a "free rider," someone who shares in the benefits of a product or service without bearing a proportionate share of the costs. We see this in "The Pledge Drive:"

Scene: Kramer is working the phones at a PBS pledge drive and Jerry is on-stage doing a spiel to ask for donations. Jerry's grandmother (Nana) sees him on her television so she calls and asks to speak to Jerry. Kramer fields her call, and asks Nana to make a donation; after all, she watches the station. Surely she doesn't want to be a "freeloader!"

Because people can watch PBS or listen to NPR anytime they wish free of charge, few actually contribute. They may value these stations a great deal but face no penalty from non-payment. Of course, if no one contributes, these stations would go off the air, and many individuals would be worse off. Society may not get the amount of public radio or television it ideally would like to have.

Non-exclusivity is one characteristic of a good that economists call a "public good." The other characteristic that defines a public good is that it is non-rivalrous, meaning that one person's enjoyment of the good does not interfere with another person's enjoyment of the same good. A fireworks display is non-rivalrous; while I am oohing and aahing, you can do the same, and I'm not any worse off for your enjoyment. By contrast, pizza is a rivalrous good: When I eat a slice of pizza, you can't eat the same slice (at least, not without making me mad).

Sometimes exclusivity and rivalrousness can be confusing. In 2015, the Woodland Town Council in North Carolina rejected a solar farm proposal because many of its citizens expressed concerns that the solar panels would absorb all of the sun's energies, leaving surrounding plants with too little sunlight to live. Ignoring the horrible science behind such claims, what was the town council suggesting about the sun's rays? They were suggesting that these rays are rivalrous, that any of the sun's rays absorbed by solar panels would not be available for use by the surrounding flora. Of course, we know that this is hogwash. But it's a great example of what being a rival good means to an economist.

As we've mentioned, public goods are both non-exclusive and non-rivalrous. One of the most common examples of a public good is national defense. It would be virtually impossible to protect the nation without this also protecting my home (whether I paid for the defense or not), making it non-exclusive. And, if I am enjoying national defense (and I do enjoy feeling secure!), that does not impede anyone else's ability to enjoy national defense as well.

It's often easy to confuse "goods that are provided by the public sector" with what economists classify as "public goods." Some goods that we may think of as public goods simply because they are provided by the government may not actually *be* public goods. Consider fire protection. If my house catches on fire, I can simply dial 911 and someone will come save it, right? But, what if you live in an area not actually covered by a city fire department? This happened to Gene Cranick, who lives in Obion County, Tennessee. Obion County does not have its own fire department, and the closest one is in South Fulton, a nearby city. The South Fulton department offers coverage to county residents for a $75 annual fee. In September 2010, Cranick's home caught fire. When he called 911, the dispatcher initially told him that help was on the way, but then called back to report that, because he had not paid his $75 fee, the fire department would not save his home. (However, they did come to ensure the fire did not spread to either of his neighbors' homes—*they* had paid *their* fee.) Apparently, fire protection can be exclusive.

How would an economist analyze this situation? Was the fire department right to deny its services to Cranick over $75? Well, the answer is a bit complicated. It is true that the loss of the family home had to have been greater than the $75 fee that went unpaid. (Cranick actually offered to pay it—and more—when the fire department refused to save his home. But to no avail—the fire department refused to accept his payment.) Thus, it appears that the fire department's decision made society worse off. But, we also need to consider how this situation would impact the future decisions of those living in Obion County. Suppose that the fire department actually agreed to save Cranick's home even though he hadn't paid. How will his neighbors behave in the future? If they are guaranteed that any fire will be extinguished whether they pay or not (if the fire protection *is* non-excludable), many of them will choose to become free riders and simply not pay. This will have a large impact on the South Fulton Fire Department's funding; they may not be able to afford as many firefighters or new equipment. This means that the decision to not save Cranick's house is likely to make society much better off in the long run.

We are used to thinking that fire protection should be provided by the government. And we are used to the idea that if the government provides fire protection, we are entitled to it. But fire protection is excludable—it has characteristics of a private good, and there's no reason it can't be provided privately. In fact, that's becoming more commonplace. In the wake of large wildfires in California, some insurance companies (such as AIG) have taken to hiring their own private firefighting forces. Celebrities Kim Kardashian and Kanye West reportedly hired their own private firefighters to save their Malibu home in 2018. Firefighting does not have to be non-exclusive, and therefore it is not always a public good.

Non-exclusivity also creates an issue in the consumption of common resources. A common resource is a resource that is non-exclusive, but rivalrous. Consider fish in the ocean. Anyone who wants to fish may do so. But each fish caught is one fewer fish available for someone else to catch, and there will likely be fewer fish reproducing in the future. Unfortunately, we may end up with fewer fish than would be best for society.

This situation is known as the "Tragedy of the Commons." It is based on a parable where a small medieval town has a pasture (called a "common") that is used for grazing sheep. Anyone in the town who owns sheep can use this area for grazing, so the common is non-exclusive. But it *is* rivalrous: When one sheep eats, that grass becomes unavailable to other sheep. Further, each sheep does some damage to the turf that the other sheep have to deal with.

Because the shepherd doesn't truly bear the full cost of his sheep grazing, his incentive is to graze more sheep on the commons than is socially ideal; as each shepherd grows his flock, the town common becomes destroyed.

Consider this scene from "The Hamptons"

> Scene: Kramer is staying at the beach with his friends. He goes down to the beach and finds a lobster trap full of lobsters. He brings them back for all of his friends to enjoy, telling them how he just found a rope and pulled it in, with a trap full of lobsters at the other end. Kramer's friend Michael is incensed. He tells Kramer that taking the lobsters is against the law. Kramer tries to calm down his friend by explaining that there are enough lobsters in the ocean for everyone.

Is Kramer right? Are there plenty of lobsters for all? Maybe not. There are two issues with what Kramer has said and done. First, those lobster traps actually belong to someone. So, he's basically taking lobsters caught by someone else. But second, if we can just pull lobsters from the sea whenever and wherever we want, there will likely not be enough for us in the future. This is just another version of the tragedy of the commons.

Kramer actually points out the problems that occur when individuals have non-exclusive access to a common resource in "The Cheever Letters:"

> Scene: Kramer arrives at Jerry's apartment a bit sad. Jerry asks him what is wrong and Kramer says he can't play golf anymore. He's been trading Cuban cigars for the right to play golf at the country club. Now he's lost the cigars, and with them, access to the course. He doesn't want to play at the public course anymore; there are too many people, too many brown patches in the grass, too many divots. And the quality of the clientele you have to play with—ack!

Kramer is sad because he no longer has access to the exclusive country club golf course, and now must play on a public course. The differences are stark—the turf, the crowds ... and (heaven forbid!) the sand traps aren't even raked! Why is the public course so rough? Because access is open to anyone willing to pay a nominal greens fee. Country clubs, in contrast, restrict membership by charging membership fees (and their greens fees are generally higher as well). Fewer people play at the country club course than at the public course, so the public course gets relatively overused.

So, how can we prevent the overuse of common resources? One way is by turning common resources into privately held goods. Think back to the town common where shepherds graze their sheep. That common could be parceled out, with each shepherd given a fenced-in area in which to graze his sheep. This changes a shepherd's incentives. Now the shepherd knows that any damage done to his turf is his own; by overgrazing, he's only hurting himself. To ensure that the area will provide a feeding ground for his flock for years to come, he cuts back his flock to a more ideal number.

Property rights encourage careful management of endangered resources. Consider the case of the black rhino. It was hunted to near extinction in Africa, with much of the reduction in the herd caused by poaching and the destruction of the animal's habitat. What may seem counterintuitive is that the creation of a trophy-hunting industry (which transferred the right to some rhinos from the government to trophy hunters) may have actually saved the black rhino from extinction. I know what you're thinking ... but it's true! Here is the basic idea: Sell a few licenses to hunt and kill black rhinos (particularly those beyond breeding age and a danger to younger rhinos) and then use the money from these sales to fund anti-poaching efforts and habitat restoration. In 2014, a Texas man bid $350,000 for a license to kill a black rhino in Namibia. It was one of 18 licenses sold that year. The criteria for the rhino that can be hunted and killed are very specific. Killing the wrong one is more than a public relations nightmare ... it can land you in prison.

In another example, villages in Africa were given "ownership" of the elephants in their region and then allowed to sell licenses to allow individuals to hunt them. This provided two incentives for the villagers. First, they had a strong incentive to protect the elephants from poachers. They didn't want to lose a commodity so valuable to them without a fight. Second, they had an incentive to be restrictive in the number of licenses to hunt that they did sell; they needed to ensure that the herd would live on and provide additional revenues in the future.

Another way that we can avoid the tragedy of the commons is to ask the government to limit access in order to ensure sustainability. We see this in many examples drawn from the natural world: The government only allows deer hunting at certain times of the year; you can only hunt male ring-necked pheasants; you can keep largemouth bass only if they've reached a certain size; you can't hunt owls at all. In fact, to ensure that rivers keep flowing, some state governments have made it illegal for households to gather rainwater in rain barrels! In each of these cases, government regulation serves to more clearly define rights to certain resources—what you have access to (and what you don't), when you have access, and how much access you're entitled to.

The key to all of these problems is the issue of property rights. Whenever property rights are ill-defined, it is likely that the economic pie is smaller than it could be. Third parties may be impacted by the actions of buyers and sellers because resources are used without proper payment. Forcing these economic actors to recognize these external costs is a way to ensure a more efficient outcome. In the case of common resources, private ownership or clearer assignment of property rights can provide the proper incentives to alleviate their overuse. So, while "sharing is caring" and seems like the *nice* thing to do, property rights actually help us use our resources in a way that ensures more economic pie for everyone. And seriously, who doesn't want more pie?

7

I AM GONNA BEAT THE HELL OUT OF THIS CAR

Markets with asymmetric information

Scene: Jerry is at a rental car agency to pick up a car. The rental car agent tells him that, unfortunately, they have no mid-size car available. Jerry is understandably confused—after all, he's made a reservation. The rental agent assures him that, yes, they have the reservation, but they ran out of cars. This is even more confusing to Jerry—doesn't the reservation hold the car? And isn't the "holding" part of the reservation the part that really matters? The rental agent then offers Jerry a compact car, a blue Ford Escort. She offers him the insurance and Jerry tells her that she'd better sign him up for it, because after he's done, that Escort's going to need some repair!

In Chapter 5, we learned that well-performing markets can't be improved upon by government policymakers. But in Chapter 6, we learned that not all markets perform well. In particular, when the good being bought and sold in the market creates external costs or benefits, those goods tend to be produced in less-than-ideal amounts.

There's another circumstance in which markets often underperform, too. They may fail to deliver on their promise when one party to a transaction has more information about the product or service trading hands than the other does. Economists have a special name for this—they call it "asymmetric information." That sounds like an opportunity for one person to exploit the other, and it can be. Consider the trade that takes place between Kramer and Newman in "The Pitch." Newman is giving Kramer a motorcycle helmet in return for a radar detector. Jerry tells Newman that he's a cheat, that a radar detector is way more valuable than a helmet. But Kramer holds firm, the deal is consummated. Once Newman leaves, Jerry asks Kramer if the radar detector even works. Kramer smiles. Nope!

Oops, Newman! He traded his motorcycle helmet for a radar detector, but unbeknownst to him, the radar detector doesn't work! We can be pretty sure that he wouldn't have made the trade had he been aware of the truth. This is where the concept of "buyer beware" comes in, especially when buying a used product.

Here, there is an information asymmetry—the seller has much more knowledge of the used good than the buyer, who can never be certain of the quality of a used product. If the good is sold without a warranty, a buyer can get stuck with a worthless good. Even worse, sometimes when asymmetric information exists, the party most open to exploitation will simply choose not to participate in order to prevent that from happening. And that can be problematic, too.

This chapter discusses a few of those difficult situations, which really touch on some of the things most important to us: How can I prevent illness or accident from turning into a financial catastrophe? How can I find the right life partner? And how in the heck can I locate a good used car?

Let's begin by talking about a product all of us will have to buy at some point or another—insurance. Buying an insurance policy is a classic example of asymmetric information: You know, for example, far more about your driving habits than your auto insurer does. But your insurer is going to have to pay for the stupid things you do, and somehow they have to figure out how much to charge you for that risk. That's a difficult problem, and it's no wonder insurance markets sometimes work poorly. And it's too bad, because insurance coverage is something most of us desire. We want it because most of us are averse to risk: We like knowing that doctor visits will be affordable; it comforts us to know that if we have an auto accident, we won't have to spend our life savings to repair our car.

To fully understand the problems asymmetric information creates in insurance markets, it's important to have a bare-bones understanding of how insurance works. Let's suppose that George, Jerry, Kramer, and Elaine are all worried about getting in a fender bender on New York City's busy streets. So, to avoid getting stuck with an expensive repair bill, they agree to contribute some money to a joint bank account that they will use to pay the cost of any accidents they have. If each person in the group has a one-in-four chance of getting in an accident annually, then on average, the group will have one accident between them each year. If an accident typically costs $2,000, then in order to fund the bank account, each will have to contribute $500 per year to cover those costs. That's an arrangement that will work well for the group—the money they contribute will, on average, cover the cost of accidents, and nobody in the group has to come up with $2,000 unexpectedly. This is basically how insurance works.

But things might look different if Kramer and George are higher accident risks than Jerry and Elaine. In that case, Kramer and George will receive more benefits than Jerry and Elaine, yet each of them will contribute to the accident account equally. Elaine, for example, might contribute $500 each year, but only have one accident every ten years; she ends up paying $5,000 over those ten years to cover $2,000 worth of repairs. Kramer might contribute the same $500, but have an accident once every two years; he pays $1,000 to receive $2,000 from the pool.

That makes Kramer and George feel like they got a great deal, and makes Jerry and Elaine feel like they've been taken advantage of. So suppose that Elaine says she'd rather not participate and drops out of the pool. In order to cover Kramer's and George's bad driving habits, the three people left have to contribute a little more to the account every year. This makes insurance look like an even worse deal for Jerry who, like Elaine, quickly leaves the group. In the end, the entire insurance scheme unravels, with only the worst risks (Kramer and George) still in the pool, and paying a lot of cash for the privilege.

This problem, in which only the worst risks have insurance, illustrates a problem economists call "adverse selection." This is exactly what happens in "The Alternate Side" when Jerry, who *knows* he's a bad risk because he plans to abuse the car, purposefully requests insurance he wouldn't likely purchase otherwise. Is it any surprise that insurance is so expensive?

Adverse selection rears its ugly head in other places, too. Consider the market for used cars. Some potential sellers have terrific used cars—we can call those cars peaches. Other potential sellers are just looking to offload the hunk of junk that's littering their driveway—we'll call those cars lemons. The problem of adverse selection arises because potential buyers can't tell a lemon from a peach. And do you really think the seller is going to tell you?

Suppose that lemons are worth $1,000, and peaches are worth $5,000, and that initially, half of the cars available for sale are lemons and half are peaches. Then, to a buyer who cannot distinguish between them, a used car ought to be worth $3,000, the average value of lemons and peaches. The problem, of course, is that sellers who have peaches don't want to sell them for $3,000; their cars are worth $5,000! So, many may take their cars off the market. And, seeing that cars are selling for $3,000, many owners of lemons come out of the woodwork to offer their clunkers for sale.

So the number of peaches available on the market falls and the number of lemons rises. But that drives down the average value of a car even further, and makes owners of peaches even more reluctant to sell. Eventually, the only cars offered for sale are lemons, and they end up selling for an honest price of $1,000. That's adverse selection at work—only the worst examples end up participating in the market.

So, adverse selection can cause insurance markets to unravel, and can destroy the market for good used cars. How can we overcome this problem? Well, the problem of adverse selection arises because of a lack of information. In insurance markets, not being able to tell which insurance applicant is a good risk and which isn't leads to a pool of individuals who are all high risk. In the used car market, not being able to tell which car is a lemon and which is a peach leaves the market with only lemons. And so, if the problem arises because of too little information, the solution may well lie in finding ways to gain more information. We'll explain how automobile dealers and insurance companies do that just a bit later. But before we do, there's one additional problem of asymmetric information that we need to explore.

Once we obtain insurance, we often find that it can be liberating. With insurance, we can relax a bit, drive more quickly or carelessly, and leave our cars unlocked (maybe even while running). After all, we're covered, right? Economists call these behavior changes a "moral hazard." Moral hazard is a concern because these changes in the way we act once we have insurance tend to make it more costly for insurance companies to provide us with the coverage.

Remember Jerry and his stinky car (caused by the valet's B.O.) that we discussed in Chapter 6? Jerry tries to sell the car because it smells so badly, but no one will buy it. So, what does he do? He parks the car in a high-crime area and he leaves the keys in it. After all, the car is insured—he has nothing to lose but the odor. Would he have chosen this option if the car was not insured? Probably not.

This is one of the problems with insurance. It causes those insured to behave in ways that would not be in their best interest if they didn't have insurance. Consider banks. The Federal Deposit Insurance Corporation (FDIC) insures customers' accounts up to $250,000. Thus, banks know that, even if they make bad loans or investments, their depositors are safe and protected. How does this FDIC insurance influence the banks' behavior? It induces them to be less wary of risks, and perhaps encourages them to take on more risk than is best for society. After all, if things go badly, their depositors will still have funds (up to $250,000) and the banks won't have to face the full costs of the risks they are taking.

Much of the financial crisis of 2008 occurred because many banks thought they were "too big to fail." In other words, banks believed that, even if they made bad decisions on loans and investments and lost everything, financial regulators would protect them and prevent them from going under. This led them to take risks that were much greater than they should have. And then, when things fell through and the economy began to tank, what happened? Some of these banks were actually saved by regulators who didn't want to see them collapse! This is exactly what these banks expected when they took on more risk than was appropriate.

Rescuing failed banks today only compounds the problem tomorrow. Bailing out banks that take on unwise amounts of risk sets a precedent that encourages banks to take on more and bigger risks in the future. After all, if the loans or investments default, the government will bail the bank out, and if the risks pay off, the banks get to reap all of the rewards.

So, how can we solve the problems associated with asymmetric information? Sometimes, when the parties to a transaction have incomplete information about one another, they will employ strategic devices designed to elicit information from, or reveal information to, the other party. Such devices are called screening and signaling devices, respectively. If effective, they can give the parties involved a bit of additional confidence when entering into any kind of transaction, including market transactions and even romantic transactions.

Screening has great value in insurance transactions. Insurers can charge you more appropriate premiums if they know what your true characteristics are, and how much additional risk you'll be willing to bear once you're insured. Life insurers, for example, ask questions about your family's medical history on your application; they do blood tests to see if you're a smoker and to check your cholesterol; they ask if you enjoy risky hobbies like skydiving. And if any of those markers for risk pops up, they jack up your premium to compensate.

Information solves adverse selection problems in the used car market, too! The reason you can still find a good used car is that there are some ways for buyers to verify the quality of the cars they buy. For example, before you buy that 1992

Nissan 300ZX you've been dreaming of, you can run the car's Vehicle Identification Number (VIN) through the Carfax website to see if it's ever been totaled in a wreck or salvaged from a flood. Or, if you're really worried about getting stuck with a lemon, you can buy a certified pre-owned (CPO) car from a dealer. That gives you more information about the car's quality: CPO cars have been inspected, repaired if necessary, and warranted against being a lemon for some time after purchase. And, of course, lemons are rejected for CPO status by the dealer; if you buy a CPO car, you're buying a peach!

In the case of automobile insurance, you may find ways to signal to the insurance company that you are a safe risk, by choosing a higher deductible or enrolling in a safe-driving class. You can now even get a device from your insurance company that tells them about your driving habits, especially whether you accelerate quickly or brake too hard and too late. Information like this helps correct the asymmetric information problem and makes the auto insurance market much more efficient.

When Korean carmaker Hyundai first started selling cars in the United States, it faced a big problem of asymmetric information: American buyers, who had never heard of the brand, were suspicious of the cars' quality. So Hyundai used signaling to inform buyers that the cars were actually high quality—it offered an unprecedented 100,000 mile powertrain warranty. This told buyers two important things: Hyundai was confident that their cars wouldn't need many repairs in that interval, and if they did happen to break down, the buyer wouldn't end up bearing the cost.

Signaling appears in other contexts, too. If you are trying to impress a date and prove you are a good catch, you may follow Jerry's example from "The Truth:"

> *Scene: Elaine shows up at Jerry's apartment as he's sorting through receipts. Jerry is being audited by the IRS: He contributed money to a charity that turned out to be fake. Elaine asks him when this occurred, as she remembers him donating to some volcano relief effort on their first date. Jerry immediately tries to change the subject, offering her a drink, and Elaine realizes the truth. She mockingly asks Jerry if he was trying to impress her. What kind of girl does he think she is—the kind who'll lose control of her animal passions just because she sees a guy write a check to a charity?*

Jerry wanted Elaine to believe that he was kind-hearted and generous, so he took a serendipitous opportunity to send a signal: Kramer asked him to donate to a charity and Jerry jumped at the chance—not because he cared about the volcano victims of Krakatoa, but because of the donation's value as a signal to Elaine.

Jerry knows that there are many ways in which a person can signal how they feel about someone else as well. In "The Deal," Jerry worries about what signal his birthday gift for Elaine might send. He tells George that no matter what he gets Elaine, she's going to be attaching some subtle meaning to it. Most years, Jerry wouldn't be as concerned, but in "The Deal," he and Elaine have pushed the boundaries of their friendship by becoming "friends with benefits." Now, with Elaine's birthday just ahead, Jerry wants to give her a gift that will make her feel special, but not *too* special. At a loss for what to buy her, he decides to wrap up

$182 in cash. Elaine is understandably unimpressed—the fact that Jerry gives her cash signals to her that he put no thought into his gift, or that maybe he doesn't really know her very well. This is not a gift you want from a significant other. An uncle or a grandparent, sure. But not the person you're sleeping with. Things go from bad to worse when Kramer gives Elaine the perfect gift, something she had discussed wanting many times.

So, signaling can help a person who has important information to convey to another party. On the other hand, if you're the party to a transaction who has the least information, you might employ a screening device to elicit that information from the other party. For example, a car insurance company will look at your driving record to screen out those who have multiple moving violations or accidents; potential romantic partners will often cyber-creep their new prospects to look for indicators of character and virtue, like a good job ... or a mugshot.

That's a very obvious way to screen for information, but sometimes screening devices are more subtle. For example, when Progressive Auto Insurance asks if you'd like to install its Snapshot Telematics device, it's screening its customers to avoid adverse selection: Safe drivers are more likely to sign up for the device; reckless drivers will opt out. Progressive may then set their premiums accordingly.

And what about romance? Is there a way we can gather information about the quality of a potential mate (beyond, that is, what you can find in a Google search)? Truthfully, this can be hard. Imagine a speed dating lunch, in which you (a bit lonely) have signed up with a service who will match you with ten people for five-minute face-to-face conversations. During those conversations, you're supposed to assess the quality of each and decide who you might want to see again.

Unfortunately, talk is cheap: In a five-minute conversation, your matches might tell you anything—about their work with the blind, about the size of their bank account, or about how they're caring for their elderly parents. And because they can tell you anything, they're really telling you nothing. To acquire really useful information, you need to be more strategic; the information you elicit must be more costly to your matches than just saying the right thing. This is why a fairy tale princess on a speed date might ask each of her potential suitors to slay a dragon for her. In the process, her princes will separate themselves into two very obvious groups: Those who are really brave and those who only say they are.

Another area in which we see signaling and screening is the hiring process. For example, firms may set up employment applications with specific questions geared to screen out unsuitable applicants. The interview process also involves screening as well. Candidates can send signals to potential employers in a variety of ways. A college degree is an example. Sure, individuals with a degree generally have more education and training than those without one. However, we do see a difference in job opportunities and incomes between someone with four to five years of college education who completed their degree program and someone with the same four to five years of college who didn't graduate. The two may have learned the exact same things in college, so why is there a difference in job opportunities and pay? Because the degree recipient is sending a valuable signal: Earning a diploma means that she can start and complete a task, jumping through all of the hoops necessary to complete her goal. Labor economists call this the "sheepskin effect" of a college degree. Most studies that examine the gains from education try to separate the effects of the improvement in productivity from earning a college degree from the signaling effect of the diploma.

So, while markets that have asymmetric information may suffer from inefficiency, some of these difficulties can be overcome. There are multiple situations in which not all parties involved in a transaction may have complete information, but signaling and screening devices can dramatically improve outcomes. Getting the "deets" helps every market participant make better decisions so they can live their best lives. And isn't that what we all want?

8

A MAN WITHOUT HAND IS NOT A MAN

Strategic behavior

> *Scene: George enters Jerry's apartment looking worried. He feels like his girlfriend is about to break up with him. Last night he asked her out for dinner, and she suggested lunch instead. This is like being demoted! And then George realizes his problem: He has no power, no "hand" in the relationship. Kramer offers a solution—George should break up with his girlfriend. George's face lights up. He considers such a preemptive breakup a brilliant strategy. There's no way he can lose!*

In "The Pez Dispenser," George is certain that his girlfriend Noel, who has not been treating him as well as she used to, is planning to break up with him. George seizes the advantage by threatening a preemptive breakup, and for a time elicits love and kindness from Noel at a level he never dreamed possible.

This chapter deals with human interactions at a more granular level than the human interactions that take place in markets. In markets, individuals are often more or less anonymous. They come to the market, they observe the prices of the various goods and services that they might be interested in purchasing, and then they make decisions that they act on before getting back in their Teslas and heading home. Nobody is pitted against them; nobody has to work with them; nobody is trying to outsmart them. In fact, now that so many restaurants have ordering kiosks and so many stores have self-checkout, consumers might never have to look another human being in the eye.

But many of the most important interactions we'll have throughout our lives are the more intimate, face-to-face encounters that take place with our spouses, our kids, or our archnemeses. The outcomes of these encounters, unlike those described in the paragraph above, depend not only on the decisions we make, but also on the decisions of the other people involved. Economists call this "mutual interdependence," which is a five-dollar phrase that means that the punishments or rewards we receive from our interactions with others depend on the decisions we make *and* the decisions made by others.

Unfortunately, the tools that economists have historically used to analyze markets aren't much good at analyzing such mano-a-mano standoffs. So, beginning in the 1940s, economists and mathematicians began developing a new theory of strategic interactions to explore such situations. That theory is called "game theory," and while it sounds like something you could use to beat your punk kids in Monopoly (and it is!), it's even more useful in manipulating your spouse into emptying the dishwasher and your offspring into getting better grades. (If you've seen Russell Crowe in *A Beautiful Mind*, you've had an introduction to game theory. In the movie, Crowe plays the role of John Nash, who won a Nobel Prize in economics in 1994 for his pioneering work in the field.)

Let's dig into the basics of game theory by analyzing a simple game. Suppose that Jerry and Elaine, having recently rekindled their romance, have plans to meet for lunch. Unfortunately, although they both recall that they're supposed to meet at noon, neither can remember where—Monk's or the bagel shop. And, because *Seinfeld* is set in the 1990s (before we humans became surgically attached to our cellphones), they have no way to contact one another to double-check on the location. If they both end up at the same place, they'll be together and happy; if they go to different places, they'll be lonely and upset.

Jerry and Elaine are playing an economic game. The outcome of the game depends on what both players do: Jerry's happiness depends on his choice (Monk's or the bagel shop), but it also depends on where Elaine decides to go. And so, this game, like every economic game, can ultimately be described in terms of who the players are, what choices are available to them, and the rewards or punishments each player might receive.

Let's summarize this information (players, choices, rewards) in a convenient table:

| | | Elaine | |
		Monk's	Bagel shop
Jerry	Monk's	1, 1	0, 0
	Bagel shop	0, 0	1, 1

You'll notice that both of our players are represented—Jerry on the left and Elaine across the top. Next to Jerry, you'll see the choices available to him: Monk's or the bagel shop, carefully aligned in rows. In fact, Jerry is often referred to as the row player, because he gets to decide which row of the table everyone will end up in. Notice that Elaine has the same choices, but that hers appear below her, arrayed in columns. Elaine is the column player; she gets to decide whether both of them will end up in the "Monk's" column or the "Bagel Shop" column.

And then there are the cells (or boxes) in the table that contain numbers. These numbers represent the rewards that Jerry and Elaine receive for the various combinations of their choices. Each of these cells contains two numbers: The first number belongs to Jerry and the second belongs to Elaine. Here, if Jerry goes to

Monk's and Elaine goes to Monk's, too, we end up in the top row and left-hand column. There, Jerry gets a reward of 1 and so does Elaine. In this game, we might consider these rewards or payoffs as "warm fuzzies" or "smiles." In other games, the numbers might represent dollars of profit or years in prison. Generally speaking, the higher the payoff a player receives the better (except, of course, when the payoffs are measured in years in prison). But all that really needs to be true most of the time is that they denote the player's ranking of all of the outcomes. In this game, we could replace the ones with one hundreds, and the zeros with tens, and the relative rankings would remain the same.

That sounds like a lot of mathematical and organizational baggage to bring to a fairly simple situation. But we'll find that in more complex situations, that system of organization can be super-useful and can bring clarity to messiness. And, even here, you'll find that the story the table tells is an interesting one, a story that is more than mere numbers. It's a story of love. Doesn't that make you feel all shmoopy?

To determine how each player will "play," consider their options. Each has to start by considering what the *other* will do. Think about this from Elaine's perspective: If she believes that Jerry will go to Monk's, she only needs to consider her payoffs in the first row of the table. She can go to Monk's and receive a payoff of one or go to the bagel shop and receive nothing. (Remember that her payoff is the second number in each cell.) Obviously, going to Monk's is the better option. On the other hand, if she believes that Jerry will go to the bagel shop, she will consider her payoffs in the second row. Going to Monk's will give her a payoff of zero; thus, going to the bagel shop is the better choice.

We can turn to Jerry's decision in the same way. If he thinks Elaine will head to Monk's, then he will compare the payoffs in the first column; he is better off going to Monk's. If he expects Elaine to go to the bagel shop, his payoffs come from the second column and he will choose to also go to the bagel shop.

The fundamental problem Jerry and Elaine face is not figuring out what they should do. The problem they face is figuring out what the *other* person is going to do, and then responding appropriately. That's more complex than it seems: Elaine has to figure out what Jerry will do, knowing that Jerry is trying to figure out what Elaine is thinking about what Jerry will do. It's pretty easy to get caught up in a downward spiral of "He thinks that I think that he thinks that I think ..." which means that the essence of game theory boils down to the problem of getting inside your opponent's head. That can be very hard to do!

We said earlier that this particular game is a story of love. Let's dig a bit deeper and see why. Notice that Jerry and Elaine's best outcomes come when both of them end up in the same place—either at Monk's or the bagel shop. And we know that Jerry and Elaine are in love because they don't care *where* they meet—they get the same rewards (one unit of warm fuzzies each) no matter where they meet. Notice further that when Jerry and Elaine fail to coordinate—when one is at one Monk's and the other is at the bagel shop—neither gets anything. They only want to be together; there's no joy in being somewhere, no matter how interesting, when you're alone. (Ah, to be young and in love ...)

In "The Barber," George faces a situation that can be modeled in a similar way:

Scene: George is at a job interview. His would-be boss Mr Tuttle tells him that he wants to hire him, but follows that up with an "of course …" before he is interrupted by a phone call. By the time George checks back in, Tuttle has left on vacation, leaving George to wonder if he, in fact, has been given the job or not. George being George, he decides to report for work on Monday as if the job has been his all along. After all, he doesn't want to lose this chance, and in the week Mr Tuttle is gone, George digs in like an Alabama tick. When he asks Jerry what could possibly go wrong with his plan, Jerry wisely points out that George could end up embarrassed in front of a large group of people. Not that that's ever stopped George before!

We can put together another table like the one above to demonstrate this "game." Here, the two players are George and Tuttle; each has choices (although they differ); and the payoffs received will depend on what each player decides:

		Tuttle	
		Hires George	*Doesn't hire George*
George	*Show up*	1, 1	-1, -1
	Don't show up	-1, -1	0, 0

Where did these payoffs come from? What story do they tell? George clearly prefers to have the job and doesn't want to be embarrassed. Therefore, he receives his highest payoff when he shows up for the job and it turns out that Tuttle wanted to hire him. On the other hand, there are two situations that would hurt George, giving him a negative payoff: Showing up when Tuttle wasn't going to hire him, and missing out on being hired by not showing up even though Tuttle wanted him. In the final case, where Tuttle doesn't want to hire George and George doesn't show up, George simply receives a payoff of zero. We can tell a similar story about the payoffs received by Tuttle.

So, what will George do? Let's work through his decision-making process. Suppose George believes that the interview went very well, and Tuttle wants to hire him. This means George should consider his payoffs in the first column. He can show up and receive 1 or not show up and receive -1. In this case, his best option is to show up. However, if he feels that Tuttle doesn't want to hire him, he needs to consider his payoffs in the second column. He can show up, be embarrassed, and receive a payoff of -1, or not show up and earn zero. Here, George wants to not show up.

There are two "no regrets" outcomes to this game—outcomes where both players are doing the best they can, given the way the other guy played. One is in the upper-left cell: Neither George nor Mr Tuttle can improve his payoff by, on his own, switching strategies. The other is in the lower-right cell; again, neither George nor Mr Tuttle can improve his payoff by switching strategies. Those no-regrets outcomes are called "Nash equilibria," in honor of the late mathematician John Nash; generally, Nash equilibria are likely places for a game to end up.

Not all Nash equilibria are created equal! Note that payoffs are best for both players when Tuttle wants to hire George and George shows up for work; payoffs are lower at the outcome where Tuttle doesn't want to hire George, and George doesn't show. Both players would prefer to end up in the upper-left-hand corner of the game.

Let's contrast this game with the game described in "The Pledge Drive" (which we discussed previously in Chapter 6). In that episode, Jerry's Nana calls the PBS pledge drive to speak with Jerry, and Kramer encourages her to make a donation. This is a game that is played every day by millions of PBS listeners. PBS, of course, relies heavily on voluntary viewer contributions to fund its programming. (Although it does receive some government funding, $6 out of every $7 comes from these voluntary contributions.) It's unfortunately super-annoying to listeners that PBS always seems to be in the middle of a pledge week; there never seems to be enough money coming in. Let's see if we can use a bit of game theory to figure out why.

		Other listeners	
		Contribute and listen	Listen for free
Nana	Contribute and listen	5, 5	2, 7
	Listen for free	7, 2	3, 3

Here's a game where incentives really matter (you *did* read Chapter 2, didn't you? If not, go back and do your homework!). If everyone contributes, PBS will have enough money to offer high-quality programming, and Nana and the other listeners will get a large benefit (5). If only one party contributes, the programming will suffer from a small lack of funding; and, if nobody contributes, PBS will have to use its paltry government allocation to come up with *something* to fill the airwaves; "The History of Kale" and "Knitting Theory" spring to mind as obvious choices.

Here's the rub in this game: Once PBS airs a broadcast for a listener who has contributed, it's also made it available to listeners who haven't contributed. Let's suppose that others have contributed. Then Nana can either contribute and enjoy super-high-quality programming, or she can choose not to contribute and settle for slightly less interesting programming. (That's why the reward to contributors falls to a 2 when Nana doesn't contribute—the other contributors have spent a lot of money to produce some marginally interesting programming.) Nana can then enjoy those programs and spend the money she saves on something else she enjoys, like booze and fireworks (that's why her reward goes up to a 7).

Of course, if nobody contributes, you get the kind of super-low-quality programming we described above, perhaps "Understanding Crabgrass." And while Nana and the others don't really love that programming, at least they're not paying for it!

What's the likely outcome of this game? One way to determine this is to examine each outcome and see if everyone is satisfied with it—in other words, look for the no-regrets outcomes, or Nash equilibria. Take, for example, the outcome where everyone contributes. Nana says to herself, "Well, I like getting a payoff of 5, but if I cancel my check, I could listen to some fairly decent programming for free and get 7." And so, Nana is unlikely to contribute, making this particular outcome unlikely.

What about the outcome where Nana contributes and the others don't? Nana gets a reward of only 2, but could, again, increase it to 3 if she'd just stop payment on her check. And what's true for Nana is true for the others, which means that the only outcome where everyone is satisfied, where nobody has any regrets or wishes to change their mind, is the outcome where nobody contributes. There, if anyone decides to spontaneously open their wallet, they make themselves worse off—their reward falls from a 3 to a 2.

So, nobody contributing is the likely outcome in this game, and it's worth noting that it's a really lousy outcome—Nana and the others end up with programs like "The Hidden Philosophy of Spinach" that they don't particularly enjoy. If Nana and the others could all agree to contribute, they'd get much better programming; in fact, the programming would get so much better that it would outweigh the cost of contributing, and everyone's rewards would rise from 3 to 5.

But such an agreement suffers from two big problems. First, it's hard to enforce such an agreement, and second, everyone (Nana included!) will likely try to cheat on it for the very reasons we've described above. Individual incentives lead the players in this game to an outcome that is in the best interest of the individual but a lousy outcome for the group as a whole.

We see this scenario played out in all kinds of places in the real world: It's in the best (financial) interest of a polluter to spew waste into the atmosphere rather than spend the money to clean it up; when everyone spews their waste into the atmosphere, you end up with Beijing-level pollution and a lot of sick people. It's in the best interest of an individual fisherman to catch as many fish as possible; when every fisherman pursues his individual interest, breeding stocks are depleted and the fishery dwindles.

The poor outcome in "The Pledge Drive" is the combined result of interesting incentives: Notice that no matter what the others do, Nana is better off not contributing. Because not contributing is always better than contributing for Nana, game theorists say that it *dominates* contributing, or that not contributing is a "dominant strategy."

We see dominant strategies described brilliantly by George in "The Pez Dispenser." Remember from this chapter's opening scene that George, worried that his girlfriend Noel is about to break up with him, seeks to turn the tables and seize control of the relationship. When Kramer suggests a preemptive breakup, George immediately sees the brilliance: If Noel was going to dump him, he salvages his dignity by breaking up first. If she wasn't planning on dumping him, his preemptive breakup establishes him as the alpha in the relationship, and Noel will give him whatever he wants. So, the preemptive breakup strategy is a good one for George. Unfortunately, as we saw in "The Pledge Drive" above, sometimes dominant strategies can lead to poor outcomes. Noel eventually becomes wise to George's machinations and dumps him. When George tells her that she can't leave him because he has "hand," she coolly responds that he'll need it.

Because of the uncertainty that is sometimes involved in predicting your opponent's decisions, strategic behavior often involves the use of threats, promises, or commitments to alter the game to a player's advantage. Consider the example above where Jerry and Elaine are supposed to meet up, but they can't remember if they were supposed to go to Monk's or the bagel shop. If neither has a strong preference for one place over the other, the pair has only a 50-percent chance of actually meeting up. To eliminate this risk, the couple could simply commit to meeting at Monk's on weekdays. This commitment eliminates the uncertainty and helps Jerry and Elaine coordinate their actions so that they are both in the same place at the same time.

The commitment in this case is what game theorists call a *strategic move*, an effort by a player outside of the actual game to alter its outcome so as to provide an advantage to that player. Here, Jerry and Elaine both want to end up in the same place; therefore, this commitment (made by either or both of them) will help gain them a higher payoff.

The commitment can be a powerful tool for changing behavior. Consider this scene from "The Soul Mate:"

> *Scene: Elaine has met a man, Kevin, who desperately wants to sleep with her. He's told her he doesn't want to have kids (which is exactly what Elaine wants to hear), but George convinces her that talk is cheap, that a guy will say anything to get a woman. He offers Elaine, as an example, the time he once told a woman that he liked to spend time with his family!*

The now-dubious Elaine is unsure what to believe about Kevin's determination not to have kids. Kevin responds by demonstrating his commitment, telling Elaine, "I got a vasectomy this morning."

Kevin's surgical procedure demonstrates something important about commitments: Sometimes we strongly commit to something today, only to have our "tomorrow self" fail to follow through. For example, consider Jerry's monologue in "The Glasses:"

> *Scene: Jerry is doing stand-up comedy at a club. He laments that he never gets enough sleep because he always stays up too late. His "Night Guy" always wants to stay up late, and never worries about getting too little sleep. That's not Night Guy's problem; that's all on Morning Guy.*

This is why New Year's resolutions so often fail, why we buy expensive gym memberships that we then neglect to use, why most people find losing weight so vexing. In "The Soul Mate," however, Kevin has taken action to make his commitment firm: He's adopted a *commitment device* that makes it very hard for him *not* to maintain his resolve.

If you have an alarm clock, you've got a commitment device that helps Morning Guy live up to Night Guy's commitments. If that's not working for your Morning Guy, you can buy an alarm clock that rolls around the room getting progressively louder until you hunt it down and ~~smash it~~ turn it off. And organizations like Stickk.com and HealthyWage.com (discussed fully in Chapter 2) are all devices devoted to helping you maintain your resolve.

Jerry makes effective use of a commitment device in "The Nose Job:"

> *Scene: Jerry is in his apartment talking about a woman he has fallen for, a woman with a horrible personality but some other attractive ... assets. He is beside himself. Anxious to remove this irresistible woman from his life, he takes her phone number from his wallet and offers it to Kramer. He knows he doesn't have the willpower to get rid of the number himself, so he begs Kramer to help him. Kramer tears it to pieces and commends him on his choice.*

Kramer has, on Jerry's request, taken an important step to help steer the economic game Jerry is playing with his girlfriend to an alternative, preferred outcome: He's cut off communication. This prevents any renegotiation (*read: Booty calls*) in which Jerry might yield to immediate temptation. To see the importance of cutting off communication in strategic moves, consider a modified version of the game we opened this chapter with:

		Elaine	
		Monk's	*Bagel shop*
Jerry	*Monk's*	3, 1	0, 0
	Bagel shop	0, 0	1, 3

In this game, you'll notice that Jerry and Elaine still want to be in the same place—the love hasn't died. But Jerry gets the most happiness when they meet at Monk's, and Elaine's best outcome is if they meet at the bagel shop. So imagine you're Jerry: You want to meet Elaine, but you want to meet her where *you* want to meet her! And she wants to meet you, but she wants to meet you where *she* wants to meet you. How can you get your way?

The answer is to make a commitment, then cut off communication so there can be no renegotiation. Call Elaine at a moment when you know she can't take your call—when she's at the gym working out, or in a meeting. Leave a message:

"Elaine: I'm going to Monk's. Meet me there!" And then … turn off your phone for the rest of the morning. Elaine will have little choice but to go to Monk's, where she gets a payoff of 1, because if she goes to the bagel shop knowing that you won't be there, she'll get a payoff of 0.

George makes effective use of cutting off communication in "The Susie:"

> Scene: George's girlfriend is about to break up with him. (Are you sensing a pattern here?) Feeling that the breakup is imminent, George tells her he is out of soda and he leaves to go get more. Then, he never returns. When Jerry later observes that George can't avoid her forever, George replies that if she can't find him, she can't dump him!

Another powerful strategic move is called the *threat*. A threat is a conditional strategic move designed to get your opponent to act in a way he otherwise wouldn't. *"If you don't behave in the way I want you to, I will punish you by doing something that harms you."* Consider, for example, the tension between the U.S. and North Korea involving missile testing by the North Korean government.

		U.S.	
		Hard line	Appeasement
North Korea	Test missiles	-1, -1	3, -2
	Don't test missiles	-3, 1	0, 2

Suppose a new U.S. president has just taken office and is considering policy options toward North Korea. The president can chum up to Kim Jung Un (appeasement) or take a hard line. North Korea has the option of continuing its missile development program or suspending it. Let's consider the options faced by Kim Jong Un. If the U.S. takes a hard line, he will want to go ahead and test missiles because that yields a higher payoff (-1 rather than -3). Alternatively, suppose he believes that the new president will take a softer stance (appeasement); he is still best off choosing to test missiles (when he tests, he gets a payoff of 3; if he doesn't, his payoff is 0). Therefore, testing missiles is a dominant strategy for Kim Jung Un because he receives a better payoff no matter what the U.S. chooses to do. Knowing this, the U. S. will adopt a hard-line foreign policy toward North Korea. This is a less-than-desirable outcome for the U.S., which prefers the outcome in which the U.S. takes a softer stance toward North Korea and North Korea doesn't test missiles.

Is there a way that the U.S. can incentivize Kim Jong Un to not test his missiles? One way would be to use a threat as a strategic move before the game even begins. Suppose the President of the U.S. announces that if North Korea tests missiles, the U.S. will create a naval blockade that will prevent shipments of goods from reaching the citizens of Pyongyang. What does this threat achieve? It alters the payoffs in the table for both the U.S. and North Korea. The blockade will hurt the people of North Korea by restricting their access to goods and services (note that North Korea's payoff in the "Test Missiles" row falls by four compared to the payoffs in the original game). The blockade is also costly for the U.S. to impose; it costs the U.S. two points if it has to use it.

| | | U.S. | |
		Hard line (and blockade if missiles)	Appeasement (but blockade if missiles)
North Korea	Test missiles	-5, -3	-1, -4
	Don't test missiles	-3, 1	0, 2

Let's consider North Korea's options, assuming for the moment that it believes the U.S. will follow through on its threat. If the U.S. takes a hard line, North Korea will be worse off testing its missiles and earning a payoff of -5, rather than simply losing face by backing down and earning a payoff of -3. If the U.S. chooses appeasement, North Korea receives -1 if it tests missiles (and endures a blockade) but earns 0 if it suspends its missile program. Therefore, the threat of a blockade, by changing the payoffs to North Korea's options, turns suspending the missile program into a dominant strategy for North Korea, and allows the U.S. to adopt a friendlier overall policy stance. The U.S. gets what it wants, and because North Korea suspends its testing program, the threat never has to be carried out.

It is important, however, that the threat be credible. North Korea must believe that the U.S. will *definitely* impose the naval blockade if it tests its missiles. And it must believe that the U.S. will *not* impose a blockade if it chooses to not test its missiles. What makes a threat credible? First, it must be costly for the U.S. to impose the blockade. This way, North Korea knows it can avoid the blockade by doing as the U.S. wishes, because the U.S. would not choose to impose the blockade otherwise. Second is to use signaling. You may remember that we discussed signaling in Chapter 7, as a way for an individual to provide information to another party to resolve an information asymmetry. For example, the U.S. could signal the strength of its commitment to its threat (and thereby increase its credibility) by moving its naval forces to the waters near North Korea.

If you decide to use a threat to turn a game to your advantage, it's important to right-size that threat. A threat that is too large—"If you don't practice piano for 30 minutes today, I'm going to chop off your hands with an axe!"—isn't credible. The punishment is so out of line with the offense that nobody would ever believe you'd actually follow through. But a threat that's too small, even if believed, won't be effective, either: "Son, if you fail to graduate college with a 4.0 grade point average, I'll confiscate your iPhone for 24 hours." For most teens, a lost day of cellphone use isn't nearly enough to motivate the kind of 24–7 studying that perfect grades require.

Consider this scene in "The Invitations" where George struggles with right-sizing a threat:

> *Scene: George is engaged to Susan, but really doesn't want to get married. He'd like to call it off, but he doesn't want to be the bad guy. In an effort to get Susan to pull the plug, he issues a threat: Sign this pre-nup or I will call off the wedding. Unfortunately, that threat proves ineffective: Susan responds with a laugh, pointing out that she makes more money that he does. The threat has no teeth, and Susan signs the pre-nup.*

The threat will only work if it costs Susan something should it be carried out. Because she is in better shape financially than George is, she actually benefits from the pre-nup. Once again, poor George has no hand.

The third strategic move is the promise: "If you do something you don't want to do for me, I will do something for you that makes you happier (but which I wouldn't ordinarily do—because in that case the promise won't be motivational). Promises clearly create an incentive for the one receiving the promise to do something they wouldn't ordinarily do: "If you get straight As in high school, I'll buy you something special." But the promise must be large enough to be motivating: "I'll buy you a Tootsie Roll" isn't a big enough incentive to motivate the amount of studying that straight As requires. And "I'll buy you a Ferrari" is likely to be too big to be believed. "I'll buy you a good used Kia" might do the trick.

As was the case with commitments and threats, the promise must be believed to be effective. But, because the promise is costly to the promisor, by its very nature it is unbelievable. And when a promise isn't believable, it will fail to motivate the desired behavior. We see this in "The Wig Master" (discussed in Chapter 2), when Elaine's new love interest, Craig, wants to sleep with her, and offers her a discount at the clothing store where he works. Jerry tells her the discount is just a ploy, that Craig has no intention of following through on his promise. He believes the promise of the discount is just a ruse to get Elaine to go out with him.

Of course, the defining feature of an economic game is mutual interdependence: Kramer (rightfully) points out that Craig may be thinking the same thing about Elaine. Perhaps Craig thinks she's only flirting with him to get a discount on the dress, and that she has no real intentions of going out with him. As we've learned, talk is cheap. After Craig promises Elaine a discount on a Nicole Miller dress, she asks the store manager for confirmation. The manager tells her that they aren't expecting any more Nicole Millers. You can bet Craig is one guy Elaine won't be sleeping with!

So, making your promises credible, believable, is important. Doing that is part of the art of game theory. For example, suppose you want to motivate your daughter to pole vault ten feet. You promise her $100 if she's successful. But … you're a notorious tightwad who'd rather walk two miles to a restaurant than feed a parking meter. How can you make this promise believable? One way might be to show your commitment to carrying through on your promise: Take a $100 bill, tear it in half, and give your daughter one of the worthless halves. Promise to give her the other worthless half (and a roll of Scotch Tape) when she hits the ten-foot mark.

Because the things most important to us—our kids, our romantic relationships, our ability to merge onto the 405 freeway at 5:13pm—are characterized largely by face-to-face (or car-to-car) interactions, understanding the mutually interdependent nature of those interactions is of great importance. Game theory gives us an entry point into a deeper understanding of human motivations and behaviors. Of course, we're most interested in getting the things that *we* value from those interactions, and grasping how we can use strategic moves—commitments, threats, and promises—to achieve those ends is perhaps the most useful part of understanding game theory. Master that art, and you'll have so much hand you'll be spilling out of your gloves!

9

$182 IS NOTHING TO SNEEZE AT

Are people always rational and is rationality the best thing?

> *Scene: Jerry and Elaine have decided to extend their relationship to "friends with benefits." Now, it's Elaine's birthday, and Jerry is stressed—he has no idea what to get her. On the big day, she opens her present from him. When she finds a roll of neatly wrapped bills inside, she's ... underwhelmed. Jerry tells her that cash is an ideal gift, because now Elaine can go buy whatever pleases her most. That's no consolation for Elaine—after all, Jerry is her lover, not her uncle! Kramer then enters with a present of his own—a bench that Elaine has been admiring. She's thrilled! Kramer is incredulous when he finds out that Jerry gave Elaine money. He tells Jerry he can't be serious—after all, he's her lover, not her uncle!*

This chapter discusses several topics at the frontier of economic science. Historically, economic theory has rested on the assumption that people are rational in their actions. This means that they gather all of the pertinent information about costs and benefits, weigh that information carefully, and proceed if and only if the benefits are at least as large as the costs.

But sometimes the conventions of culture can trump rationality. In "The Deal," Jerry gives Elaine what most economists would say is a perfect gift: Cash. After all, economic theory suggests that nobody knows better how to satisfy Elaine's desires than Elaine herself. But Elaine is offended that Jerry, unlike Kramer, did not put apparent effort or thought into his gift. She would have been happier receiving a gift she *didn't* like rather than enough cash to buy herself something she did! Does that sound rational to you?

There are many situations in which humans systematically fail to act rationally, and in those instances, we sometimes achieve undesirable outcomes. Human beings do not always act as the calculating, self-interested rational actors that economic theory assumes they do. Several economists, including Dan Ariely, Daniel Kahneman, and Richard Thaler have devoted their careers to understanding this contradiction. This chapter will highlight some of their work. Of course, sometimes individuals behave *too* rationally which can also produce undesirable results. One such example occurs in the episode "The Calzone:"

> *Scene: Jerry and George are having a bite at Monk's diner. George laments that the cashier at the calzone place he frequents didn't see him drop a buck in the tip jar. He tells Jerry that tipping is worthless if nobody sees it. A cynical Jerry asks if that means George won't give to the blind. Only change, never bills, the ever-practical George replies.*

This episode illustrates the two important concepts from the chapter. The first, of course, is the irrationality of tipping—particularly when dining at a restaurant to which you'll never return. It's a nice thing to do, but there is little economic reason to do it. After all, if the tip is an incentive to provide better service, it ought to be discussed at the *beginning* of the meal, not the end. The second concept this scene illustrates is that individuals often have hidden motivations that are meaningful to them, but which are not readily apparent to others. George really enjoys the appreciation he gets from the people he tips. Later in "The Calzone," in fact, he actually removes a dollar tip from the tip jar when the cashier fails to see him put it in. George intends to re-tip the dollar when the cashier's eyes are on him. But the server turns toward George at just the wrong moment and catches him with his hand in the metaphorical cookie jar; he ends up being barred from the restaurant.

We've already explored, in this book, some instances of irrationality. One big irrational bias that people fall victim to is the sunk cost fallacy, as we discussed in Chapter 2. As we learned in that chapter, you can't get sunk costs back, no matter how hard you try: Sunk costs are sunk. And so rational behavior dictates that we ignore them and try to make the best we can of things looking forward. Just because you bought 200 shares of AIG at $1,600 each in 2002 doesn't mean that you need to hang onto those shares today, with a share of AIG selling for $50. AIG plummeted for a reason, and there's no point in hoping it will someday hit $1,600 again—in the meantime, there are other stocks you could be buying with the money you've got tied up in AIG.

Elaine falls victim to the sunk cost bias in "The Strike," when she continues to eat sub sandwiches that she dislikes in hopes of getting a free one. After 23 bad subs, she only needs one more. Jerry advises her that eating that last sub is like staying to watch the end of a bad movie; that Elaine should just walk out. But Elaine won't listen. George clings to sunk costs, too, in "The Stock Tip." Having made an investment on an insider tip that has been falling, falling, falling, Jerry decides to sell his shares and move on. But not George—he's keeping those shares, holding on to the bitter end.

Lots of people cling to their long-term investments (both financial and romantic), investments that stand little hope of panning out, simply because they fall victim to the sunk cost fallacy. Remember the viral social media mantra: Don't cling to a mistake just because you spent a long time making it! (Or, be like Elsa in *Frozen* and "Let it go.")

Clinging to sunk costs is just one example of irrational behavior. Of course, there are many other forms our irrationality takes. People do crazy things, like lighting cigars with hundred-dollar bills, and signing up to be guests on *The Jerry Springer Show*. That kind of irrationality is unpredictable, random, and therefore economic science doesn't have much to say about it. But there are other irrational tendencies that appear with enough frequency and regularity that economists have begun to study them to figure out what the heck is going on. This is the focus of the field of behavioral economics.

One such tendency is the notion of anchoring. Anchoring occurs when we refer to psychological benchmarks about the value of the things we buy and give those largely irrelevant benchmarks disproportionate weight in our decision to buy or not to buy. The better the price we find relative to the anchored value, the better the "deal" we perceive we get, and the more likely we are to buy.

The odd anomaly in anchoring is that we often let the seller determine the anchor! In "The Soup Nazi," Elaine admires an armoire and asks how much it is. The seller responds by creating an anchor and then offering her a discount: "I was asking two-fifty, but you got a nice face. Two even." Elaine feels the tug of a deal in the making, idly musing that she'd always wanted an armoire ...

That strategy—set a high price as an anchor and then offer a deep discount—is common in the real world. Consider JCPenney, one of the United States' best-known soft-goods retailers. JCPenney made a practice of setting relatively high prices for its clothing and linens, and then having weekly sales in which many items were offered at substantial discounts. Frequent sales pleased JCPenney's customers—they always knew that if they waited two or three weeks, they could find their Levi's 501s marked down from $50 to $35.

And then JCPenney hired a new CEO who thought the company was spending too much money and time marking stuff up just so it could mark it back down again. He reoriented the company's pricing strategy to eliminate sales in favor of "everyday low prices." In other words, everything got cheaper! And you'd think JCPenney's customers would have enjoyed having everything be less expensive, all the time ... but they didn't. Sales dried up, the CEO was canned, and JCPenney resumed its practice of setting extra-high prices just so it could mark them down again.

To an economist, cheap jeans are cheap jeans. If Levi's are worth buying at $35 on sale, they should be worth buying if $35 is the regular price. But many ordinary people are different to economists: To them, jeans marked down from $50 to $35 is a more tempting deal than the same jeans marked at $35 every day. That type of customer allowed JCPenney to anchor the value of the jeans at the high price; when they saw a price lower than the anchor they were motivated to buy.

The notion of anchoring is used often by marketers. Gas stations, for example, often charge different prices for gas depending on whether you pay cash or use your credit card, because the credit card companies charge the gas station an extra fee. Gas stations were quick to discover that it's better to price gas high and offer a discount for cash (making some customers feel like they've gotten a good deal) instead of setting a low anchor and penalizing some other customers by charging extra for credit.

Anchoring results in some visibly irrational behaviors. For example, you probably know someone who is more motivated by getting a good deal than by the product they got the deal on. One of your authors' mothers often served dinner dishes nobody liked because she got such a great deal on liver and canned asparagus. People like that are particularly vulnerable to anchors, as "The Parking Garage" shows. In this episode, George reminisces about his father's shopping trips for used cars, trips that would have him away from the house for weeks at a time, journeying from state to state like a candidate stumping for votes. Getting a good deal was really, really important to Frank Costanza.

That devotion to the "deal" creates some paradoxical behaviors. I bet you know somebody who has driven across town to take advantage of a "$10 Off" sale on some small item like an alarm clock. Yet, that same person is unlikely to drive across town to save $10 on a new car. But ... what's the difference? In the first instance, it's worth $10 to drive across town, and in the second it's not? Ten bucks is ten bucks whether you're saving it on a pair of shoes or a Ferrari. The key, of course, is the anchor: People will drive for the alarm clock because the price is so much lower than the anchor; they won't cross town for the car because $10 off a Ferrari isn't that great of a deal. And Frank Costanza, he wanted the great deal so badly that he'd spend weeks trying to find it!

Anchoring often rears its ugly head in resale markets. Consider the television show *American Pickers*. In each episode, two guys (Mike and Frank) drive around and visit people who may (or may not) have collectibles or interesting things for sale. Many of these people have barns or storage sheds full of stuff piled up. They don't even know what is in there! But, when Mike or Frank find something buried that they'd like to buy, suddenly that item becomes invaluable to the owner. "I'll give you $20 for this dirty corn shucker you had buried underneath that pile of rubbish." "$20?" the owner replies. "That thing is worth at least $200!" Never mind that the seller hadn't even remembered that he owned it in the first place.

If you've ever held a yard sale or sold something on craigslist, you might have seen anchoring work in the opposite way. You price an item at $1. No matter what it is or what it might actually be worth, a potential buyer will try to negotiate the price down. "I see you've priced your 1961 Ferrari 250 GT California at a dollar. Would you take 75 cents for it?" Buyers in these markets often believe the price of $1 is a *starting* point, not an ending point; it will only be a *deal* if they can get you to reduce the price.

Here's another form of irrationality related to the *American Pickers* example. Suppose your all-time favorite rock band is playing a concert near you, but the concert sells out and in the very active resale market, the tickets are way out of your price range. Then, your local radio station has a contest for a pair of front row seats! All you have to do is call in; if you're the ninth caller, the tickets are yours. You wait by the radio with bated breath, the moment finally arrives ... and you win! Exciting, right? Now, what do you do with your tickets? Would you ask your best friend to head to the show? Or would you head to the resale market and sell those valuable tickets for the going price—$3,000?

Let's start by asking what an economist would do. (Note: One of us isn't sure she'd act as an economist in this case …). You weren't willing to pay $3,000 to buy these tickets—they weren't worth it. So, if you value $3,000 more than the tickets, shouldn't you want to sell the tickets you won and get $3,000 in return? After all, the choice is, once again, between having $3,000 in your pocket or seeing the show from the first row. A rational economist would sell the tickets in a heartbeat.

However, not everyone would sell the tickets. After all, it's your favorite band! And these tickets are free! Having the tickets in hand actually makes them seem a bit more valuable to you. Behavioral economists call this the endowment effect. In this case, an individual may place a higher value on keeping something he owns than he would have paid to acquire it. After all, a bird in the hand is worth two in the bush, right?

Remember in Chapter 6, when we discussed "The Parking Space?" Why was George so adamant that the space was his? Because his car was halfway in. He didn't want to let the space go—no matter how irrational he seemed. It was his! Once he decided the space was his, the value he placed on the parking space rose, and neither threats nor logic could make him move. That is the endowment effect.

In October 2018, the Powerball jackpot reached $700 million. A reporter from *Business Insider* ran a simple experiment: She stood outside a mini-mart and offered to buy the lottery tickets that exiting customers had just purchased for twice as much as they'd paid. Of the 14 people she talked with, 11 refused. *What?* They could take her money, go back inside, and buy *twice* as many chances to win! But once they had their tickets in hand, those numbers were *their* numbers. They couldn't risk giving their winning ticket to someone else, no matter the price. The endowment effect strikes again!

Interestingly, we could use this irrationality to incentivize others. As we mentioned above, it seems strange that tipping comes after the meal. So, consider the following: You sit down at a table, pull $5 out of your wallet and tell the waiter, "This is the tip you will receive if I get good service. If the service isn't good, I will leave less—or possibly even nothing." Given our social norms, the waiter may think this is rude. Who knows—he may even spit in your drink before bringing it to your table. But this strategy should work to motivate him. The waiter knows the $5 is his if he follows through with good service. And the endowment effect tells us he values keeping the $5 received at the beginning of a meal more than he values earning $5 at the end of the meal. A waiter who offers bad service, in effect, ends up paying the customer for that bad service. The endowment effect may just prevent that from happening.

A related concept (and another form of irrationality) is the idea of mental accounting. This happens when we place our money into separate mental accounts and refuse to move it from one account to the other, even though we might need to, and even though the money is totally fungible. Let's go back and think about those concert tickets. You purposefully didn't buy them for $3,000 in the resale market, even if you had the money sitting in your checking account. That money is in your account for some reason—a rainy day, a future trip to Venice, retirement. But, when you win the tickets, you actually have another $3,000 in your hand. However, even though $3,000 is $3,000, you might view the "free" money differently. You didn't have it before. Therefore, you might not use it in the same way. It hasn't been earmarked, so you feel more able to spend it on the concert (by not selling the tickets).

One of the authors of this book regularly falls prey to mental accounting. He likes to keep a small stash of "just in case" cash in a safe. Like most of us, sometimes his month outlasts his money. And rather than dip into his "just in case" money temporarily, he leaves that money alone ... and borrows the money he needs from his credit card company. Interest payments are the cost of his irrationality.

But paying a bit of credit card interest in exchange for a bit of mental accounting pales in comparison to the price mental accounting extracts on the strip in Las Vegas. You probably know (or have heard of) someone who vacationed in Vegas and found himself ahead by tens of thousands of dollars after a run of good luck, only to lose it all on a single spin of the roulette wheel. What a great story he'll have to tell back at work on Monday: "I didn't come with it; I don't have to leave with it. It was found money," he'll say, while everyone admires his devil-may-care attitude and pats him on the back. But just think what those people would say if the gambler, instead of risking "found" money, had cashed in $60,000 of his 401(k) and wagered it on one turn of the wheel. "Fool!" they'd say. Mental accounting has made a chump out of our gambler: Money is money, no matter whether you earned it in 30 minutes playing blackjack or over a lifetime of working for the man. It all spends the same. There is no such thing as "found" money!

Both in business and in their personal lives, many people fall victim to another systematic bias: Overconfidence. This rears its ugly head in situations where we might have a good outcome or might have a bad outcome. We think that the stocks we buy will go up more than they go down; we overestimate the likelihood of winning the lottery. We even overestimate our own abilities.

Consider health and fitness. Every December 31st, millions of Americans promise themselves that next year, they'll lose weight and get fit. And so, on January 1st, gyms are packed with applicants signing up for memberships. But what happens to those members in the months to come?

Consider how many gyms structure their prices. Most gyms will ask you to either sign a contract for a monthly fee—maybe $60—or you can pay as you go, at maybe $20 a visit. And, as it turns out, most people believe they'll use the gym more than the three times a month it takes to make the monthly plan worthwhile. And most people are wrong: They only use the gym a few times before returning to their old habits. Gym owners are no fools—they take advantage of this! Using detailed records of gym membership and attendance, economists have shown that most gym members would spend far less if they'd pay the seemingly high per-visit fee rather than paying what appeared to be a low monthly rate. Overconfidence costs those gym members a lot of money.

You may have fallen victim to overconfidence without realizing it. How many of you have ever taken advantage of a teaser price on a subscription box service (or, for us old-schoolers, the Columbia Record Club), planning to cancel your subscription once you got your paws on the deeply discounted first shipment, and confident in your ability to do so. And then, months later, having failed to follow through on your plans to cancel, you're struggling to return the unwanted items the subscription service has sent you. Or, worse yet, you're paying for items that you don't like and will never use. You've been hoisted on your overconfidence petard—and the subscription service is making bank!

In "The Foundation," overconfidence costs J. Peterman a lot of money too. Newly appointed to run the company, Elaine places a piece of clothing she adores—the Urban Sombrero—on the cover of the J. Peterman catalog. And when the sombrero tanks, Elaine blames Kramer for telling her that she had the skills and judgment to run the company. Kramer, abashed, acknowledges that he overestimated her abilities. Elaine has fallen victim to overconfidence, and it ultimately ends up costing her the presidency of the company: The lack of success of the Urban Sombrero prompts J. Peterman to return from Burma and demote Elaine.

So, economists do understand that people can sometimes act in ways that aren't rational. However, many of these behaviors are still predictable—we see them occur over and over. It is important to remember that economics is about how people make decisions, and understanding why people make the choices they make (however irrational those choices may seem) is an important part of what economists do. Of course, we may never fully understand some of the things that *Kramer* does, but for the most part people (including George, Jerry, and Elaine!) do behave in ways that can be explained by a decent economist. With nine chapters' worth of economics behind you now, you should feel comfortable including yourself in that distinguished group!

Now, we will move onto a short epilogue to finish up our look into the economics of *Seinfeld*. And, because you have already invested hours reading this book, you just *have* to read the next chapter to see how it ends, right? (You *almost* fell for it didn't you?)

EPILOGUE

You've read the book and yada...yada...yada..., you're now an economist!

Seinfeld first aired in 1989, and ended its run in 1998 as the most popular sitcom of all time. The show played a key role in NBC's dominance in Thursday night ratings with its "Must See TV" programming. Since leaving the air, it is estimated that the series has earned over $3 billion in syndication fees and DVD sales. The show has exhibited popularity and staying power unequalled by any other television series. As of 2020, decades after it ended its run, *Seinfeld* still airs daily on TBS.

We hope you've enjoyed revisiting some of *Seinfeld*'s greatest moments with us (if you would like to watch the scenes that we have described, you can at http://yadayadayadaecon.com). And we hope you've learned a little bit about economics using *Seinfeld* as a lens. Our guess is that neither Jerry Seinfeld nor Larry David thought one bit about the role that economics plays in each of these episodes. But, let's return to Alfred Marshall's definition of economics: the study of men in the ordinary business of life. Given that *Seinfeld* is often characterized as a "show about nothing," is there a better way to describe what Jerry, George, Elaine, and Kramer are doing in each episode than just going about the ordinary business of life? We don't believe so, and hope you agree.

Sincerely,
Alan and Linda

INDEX

adverse selection 51–52, 54
alternatives, make choices between 3
American Pickers (television show) 71
anchoring 70–71
anti-poaching efforts 48
Antitrust Division of the Department of Justice 25
Ariely, Dan 68
asymmetric information 49–52; and inefficiency 55; problems 50–53, 55
automobiles: dealers 51; insurance 53
auto safety 11

bad loans 52
bailing out banks 52
bankruptcy 14
Beautiful Mind, A 57
behavioral economics 70
benefits 37, 40
black market 31, 34
brand loyalty 27–28
bribe 43
Brinig, Margaret 12
Buffett, Warren 19
Business Insider 72
buyer beware 49–50
"buying American" 21
"buying local" 21

capitalist 14
Caring Capitalism 35
carrot and stick 11–12, 15, 17

certified pre-owned (CPO) cars 53
Chicken Tax, 1960 20
Cohen, Ben 35
collateral damage 41
commercial vans 20
commitments 66; contract 13; device 63
common resource 46
competing opportunities 7
competition 23
competitiveness 24–29
conditional strategic move 64
consumers' willingness to pay 15
cost 40
Costanza, Frank 71
cost–benefit analysis 8–10, 13, 15, 32, 37
costs 37
Cranick, Gene 45
criminal activity 13–14
cultural tradition 30
cutting off communication 63–64

DeBeers 24
decision-making 1, 9, 59
desirability and availability 2
diamond market 24
disability grants 15
Dixit, Avinash 32, 36n1
drug gangs 25

economic pie 24
economics 68, 70
economics: behavioral 70; defined 1

endangered resources 47
estimated cost 6
exchange 16, 19; gain from 17; satisfaction from 18; voluntary 20
exclusive franchise 25
exclusivity 45
explicit cost 6
external benefit 40
external costs 38, 44, 49
externality problems 44

Facebook 25
fair-minded individuals 35
"fair trade" coffee 36
Food & Drug Administration (FDA) 33
Federal Deposit Insurance Corporation (FDIC) 52
Federal Trade Commission (FTC) 25
financial crisis of 2008 2, 52
financial incentives 12–13
first-class mail 26
"first-come first-served" basis 34
Ford Motor Company 20
foreign competition 19
foreign-made trucks 20
free exchange 30
free riders 44, 46
Friedman, David 19

game theory 57
global warming 40
government intervention in market 30
gym fees 73

habitat restoration 48
Harley-Davidson motorcycles 21
Hart, Mary 39
high-quality programming 60
hiring process 54
human interactions 56

immunization 40
implicit costs 6; *see also* opportunity cost
imprisonment 31
incentives 10–12, 14–15, 33; employers use 10–11; financial 12; individual 61; insurance companies use 11; romantic 12
information asymmetry 49–50, 65
insurance: companies 46; markets 50–51; scheme 51–52
interest payments 73
interference 37
international trade and exchange 19
investment 69
irrationality 69–70

JCPenney 70

Kahneman, Daniel 68
Kenny Rogers Roasters! 38
Knee Defender 42

Landsburg, Steven 10
less-than-desirable outcome 64
Levitt, Steven 13
licensing 33
life insurers 52

Mackenzie, Richard 26
mandatory seatbelt laws 32
marketable commodity 42
market-based system 14
markets: black market 31, 34; diamond market 24; government intervention 30; insurance 50–51; power 28; private market 37; soybean market 21; under-performance of market 49; without restrictions 34
Marshall, Alfred 1, 75
Marvell, Thomas 13
membership fees 47
mental accounting 73
Metropolitan Transportation Authority 5
Miller, Nicole 66
money 5–6
monopoly 57; competition 27–28; power 24–28
Moody, Carlisle 13
moral hazard 51
movie theaters 27
mutual interdependence 56, 66

Nash, John 60
Nash equilibria 60–61
national defense 45
National Public Radio (NPR) 44–45
negative externalities 38–41, 43; notion of 39; *see also* positive externalities
Netflix 27
network goods 24–25
non-exclusivity 45–46; access to resource 46; resources 44

Odom, Bob 33
opportunity cost 3–5, 32; importance of 5–7; lower 18; relative 18–19

patent system 25
patriotic gesture 21

payoffs 64–65
Peterman, J. 74
Pigou, Arthur 41
Pigovian tax 41
positive externalities 40–41; *see also* negative externalities
prices 11; ceiling 33–34; discriminators 26; price-sensitive customers 27; regulation by government 33
private costs 38
private market 37
Progressive Auto Insurance 54
property rights 41–42, 47–48
psychological benchmarks 70
public good 45
punishments 12–15, 57; *see also* rewards

rational individuals 38
Rawlings-Blake, Stephanie 44
raw materials 20
rearranging goods 16
Redbox 27
relative opportunity cost 18–19
rent control 33, 34
retaliatory tariffs 21
rewards 12, 15; *see also* punishments
Rhodes, Cecil 24
Ricardo, David 18–19
risk of fines 31
rivalrousness 45
robotics 19
romantic relationship 4–5, 12
Rowling, J.K. 19

safety regulations 32–33
scalping 35
scarce resources 3
scarcity 2–3, 7, 32; benefit from 42; conditions of 5, 10; desirability and availability 2; importance of 3
screening devices 52
Seinfeld 75; "Baby Shower, The" 10; "Barber, The" 27–28; "Café, The" 14, 28; "Calzone, The" 69; characters 1; "Cheever Letters, The" 47; "Chicken Roaster, The" 37–38; "Chinese Restaurant, The" 4; "Contest, The" 8–9; "Deal, The" 53, 68; "Foundation, The" 74; "Glasses, The" 62; "Good Samaritan, The" 39; "Hamptons, The" 46–47; and human behavior 1; "Maestro, The" 27; "Mango, The" 14; "Nose Job, The" 63; opportunity cost 3–5; "Parking Garage, The" 71; "Parking Space, The" 42; "Pez Dispenser, The" 56, 61; "Pledge Drive, The" 60–62; scarcity 1–3; "Shower Head, The" 30; "Smelly Car, The" 39; "Soul Mate, The" 62–63; "Soup, The" 3–4; "Soup Nazi, The" 23–24, 70; "Stall, The" 1–2; "Stock Tip, The" 69; "Strike, The" 9, 69; "Susie, The" 64; "Switch, The" 4–5; "Truth, The" 54; "Wig Master, The" 12, 66
self-control 8
self-interested rational actors 68
severity of punishment 13
sex offender registry 39
sexual revolution, 1960s 12
sharing tables 17
signaling 52, 53–54, 65
Smith, Adam 17
social custom 35
social goals 15
solar farm proposal 45
Soup Nazi 23–26, 70
soybean market 21
specialization 17, 19–20
strategic interactions 57
StubHub 35
sunk costs 9, 69–70
sustainability 48
switching strategies 60

TANSTAAFL (*there ain't no such thing as a free lunch*) 3, 5, 7, 21
tariffs 20; engineering 20–21; foreign-produced commercial vans 20; on imported goods 20; on international trade 30
tax credit 11
taxpayers 37
tax policy 11–12
Thaler, Richard 68
threat 64, 66
Ticketmaster 35
time 4, 6–7, 19
trade and exchange 16, 19; gain from 17; satisfaction from 18; voluntary 20
trade-offs 3–4, 7, 25
Tragedy of the Commons 46–47
transaction cost 43
Transit Connect 20
Tullock, Gordon 11

U.S. Postal Service 26
user agreements violations 10

vaccinations 40
Volkswagen 20
voluntary transactions 23

Wealth of Nations, The (Smith) 17
weight loss bet 13

Why Popcorn Costs So Much at the Movies (Mackenzie) 26–27

zero-sum game 19
Zimbabwe, 2008 economic crisis 2, 52